A Woman's Ladder To Success

Is Paved With Broken Glass Ceilings

Diane Dutton

ESO Publications
8275 S. Eastern Ave.
Las Vegas, Nevada 89123-2591
www.WriteBooksToday.com

Cover Design: Karey Crowl, Greenbaum Marketing
Author's photo: Randy Becker Photography
Copyeditor: Sharon K. Garner
Interior Design: J. L. Saloff

Fonts: Garmond Premier Pro, Goudy Old Style
First Edition

Dutton, Diane
A Woman's Ladder to Success Is Paved with Broken Glass Ceilings

10-Digit ISBN: 0-9791521-0-0
13-Digit ISBN: 978-09791521-0-8
Library of Congress Control Number: 2006910928

Printed on Acid Free Paper in the United States of America

1.0

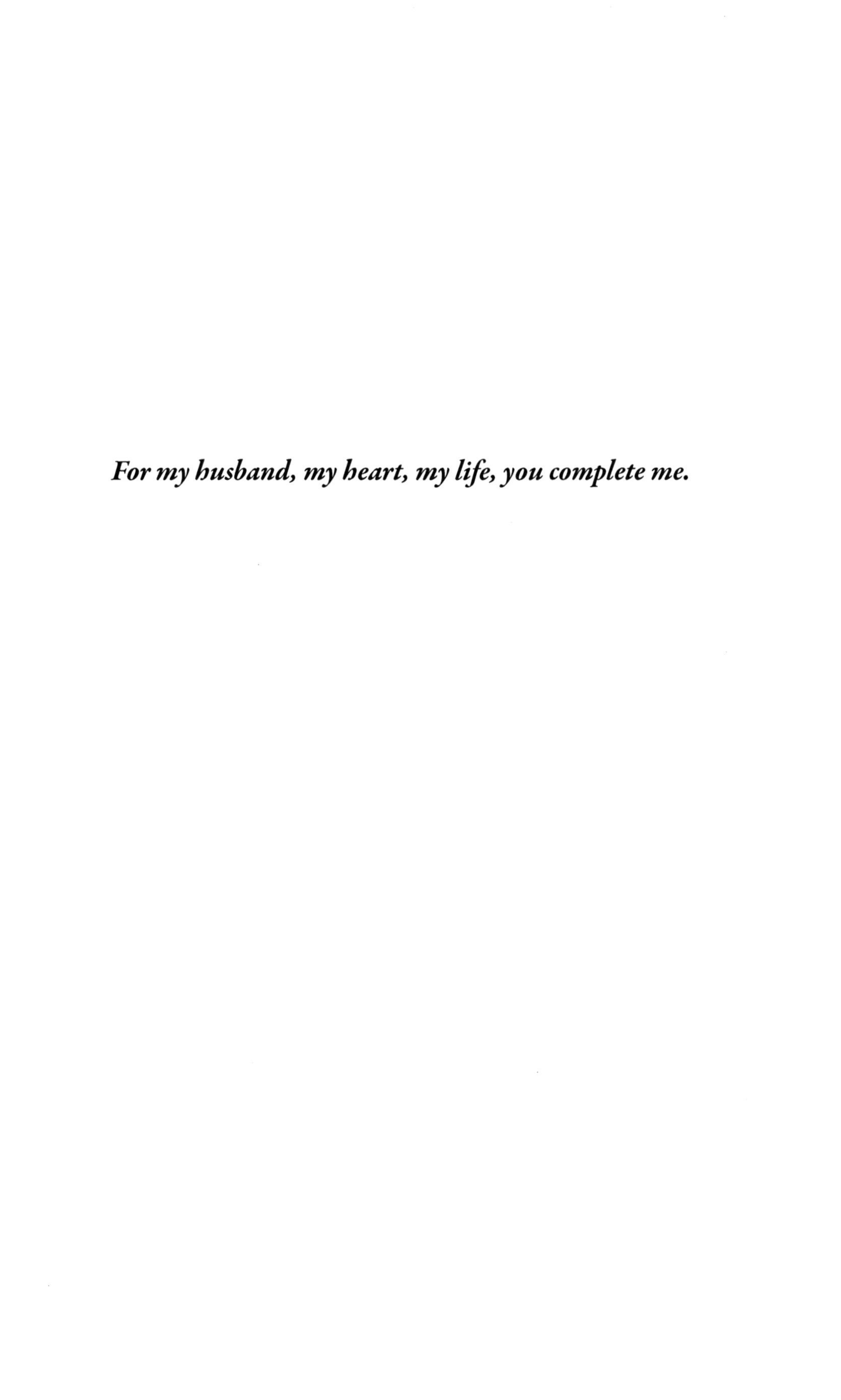

For my husband, my heart, my life, you complete me.

Table of Contents

Part I: The Journey

Step One

Step Two

Step Three

Step Four

Step Five

Part II: The Arrival

Appendix

Part I: The Journey

STEP ONE

CAN IT POSSIBLY END IN SUCCESS?

THE END AND THE BEGINNING

"...I want to thank you all for the opportunity to speak to you about the importance of core values and principles within corporate America. Those who believe men and women can break through the glass ceiling of leadership positions without a strong foundation in the fundamentals of leadership, guided by core values and principles, are quickly shown the door in today's high-pressure corporate boardrooms. The days of the Slick Willy CEO's are gone and I, for one, am happy to celebrate their demise!

So look into your hearts and minds, find your core and let it guide your passion. You will find, by looking in the mirror, you are looking at the seeds of tomorrow's great leadership.

Passion, Core Values and Core Principles should radiate from within, to our work life and to our home life. In everything we do and everything we are, the words Passion and Core should ring out clearly in our hearts and minds. As we move through our lives and our careers, don't forget this; keep it with you as you pursue excellence in your future..."

"Thank you so much for your attention, and if there are any questions, I will be available during the reception."

Applause rang out through the lecture hall as the participants showed their appreciation for the speaker's thoughts. Many years of experience had brought her to this point, to this event, to this moment in history....

Dean of the Graduate School of Management, Professor George Masters rose to his feet and joined her at the podium. He said "You are all welcome to join us at the Westgate Symposium Hall for a cocktail reception in honor of our guest lecturer today, Ms. Jesse Stevens."

The room was filled with over 1,000 students, colleagues, reporters and others in academe, all present to hear what she had to say. Pretty amazing when you think of the road she took to success. I wonder how many would never have predicted this outcome. Why? Well, not every career that starts out in the profession of accounting brings the professional to this pinnacle of success. This woman, born under the sign of Leo the Lion, the leader, was not just an ordinary accountant.

Jesse walked through the university hallways on the way to the reception being given in her honor. It's not every day that a business college graduate can make a profound impact on her peers, mentors and students. Using the accounting profession as anything more than a road to CFO or CEO was unusual at best. This renowned author and lecturer had run the accounting gamut and landed somewhere outside the standard positions of the profession. Many times our writer longed to be recognized, but not in the traditional ways most CFOs were seen. She didn't want to spend her time running the numbers and quoting Financial Accounting Standards, twenty-six years of that were quite enough for her taste. So how do you transcend the everyday accounting profession? Well, what does everyone say? "Write a book!"

So, as the days got longer and the CFO work got more stressful, the nights were filled with pages and pages of issues that face women in her profession. But one overarching vision kept creeping into her mind and then finally on to paper:

How Did I Ever Break Those Glass Ceilings?

She had started twenty-six years ago, with the naive notion that being a college graduate, an MBA no less, should grant her some special privileges in the world of the, then, Big Eight (in the late 70's) Accounting. Rude awakening; it doesn't. You are just like the rest of the pack, they said.

Wow, that first day, the Big Apple! New York City, what better place to start this exciting career in accounting with the big boys.

Jesse started out as a young, impressionable female in a man's world. After all, by most standards, Jesse was an attractive young lady. Only standing 5'1", she always wore high heels to give herself some presence. Her slim build and short, sassy haircut turned heads as she walked through the streets of midtown Manhattan. She, of course, didn't notice the looks. She was never aware of how her eyes smiled when she spoke. Only many years later would she hear, from her loving husband, what an amazingly attractive woman she is!

In the late 70s only 20% of students joining the accounting profession were women. Jesse noticed during her time in the MBA program at that prestigious business university, Pace, the commuter college located in downtown Manhattan, women were just arriving at the conclusion that accounting might be the wave of the female future. Oh, the commuter college thing? Jesse's Mom and Dad didn't want her to go away to school; after all a young woman alone needed to live at home until she got married, that's what Dad said.

So joining the very prestigious Peat Marwick Mitchell, Big Eight CPA firm, was just the ticket to the big time. She would meet important people and maybe be a partner someday. This thought quickly left her mind when she found herself as one of twelve staff members on a very large audit of a very large investment firm. The days and nights were a blur, and she learned the hard way what was important. Head down, do the work, don't give your opinion. The recurring theme throughout the years? "Don't give your opinion!"

How often have women heard "Don't give your opinion"? Just too many times for this young woman's taste. In 26 years, through nine different companies, in public accounting and private industry, public companies and private ones, large management teams and small alike, the theme remained the same: Why were they not listening? The uncanny thread of this look back at history—if you took all the recommendations Jesse had made over the years and followed the history of those executive decisions that were made against Jesse's recommendations, a significant 94% were the wrong choice!

"I should have listened to you more often," said one executive to Jesse the other day. "You just seemed to have a keen sense of what we should do, and I didn't listen to you when I should have."

Wow, did that really hit home! Jesse had given so much advice, company by company, year by year, and did they listen? The answer is no, not when it really meant giving credibility to a woman in a powerful position. Not when it meant listening to a woman over a man.

This is not unusual. Look at the statistical data. In 2005, the Federal Glass Ceiling Commission (Do you believe there really was a commission established by the government to look into this problem? What won't the government establish a commission to look at?) released a report stating that only 7-9% of senior managers at Fortune 1000 firms are women. (Korn-Ferry and Catalyst). A recent survey also noted that less than 1% of CEOs see the development of high-potential women as a priority. According to Mauricio Velasquez, Training Specialist, Diversity Training Group, women make up almost half the nation's workforce. Highly educated and/or experienced women face their biggest challenges at upper levels of corporations. As a result, they have been known to disproportionately cluster in "white-collar ghettos" of the bottom tiers of management.

According to an article in *The Economist*, July 2005, progress to break the glass ceiling is very slow, and diversity programs are not making significant headway to assist with these problems, although when women do find their way to top executive positions, it really makes a difference. Research by Catalyst, an American organization that aims to expand "opportunities for women in business," found a strong correlation between the number of women in top executive positions and financial performance among Fortune 500 companies between 1996 and 2000.

One thing we know for sure from every study, and with Women in Leadership companies popping up everywhere, you cannot legislate morality or emotional bias or diversity at the top! You cannot legislate the forcing of a company to promote a woman into senior management. Women must

MEN
CORPORATE
LADDERS →
WOMEN
ROBERT THOMPSON.

change their behavior and understand the playing field, in order to make a difference and break the glass. The change will happen when women:

- ✔ Are Trusted
- ✔ Obtain the Position
- ✔ Come From Strength
- ✔ Remain Humble
- ✔ Have Confidence Once They Reach the Top

Now let's explore the motivation behind the male executive ego, its thought process and its deep-seeded rationale for not listening to the female in business and for not promoting the female in business—and why the glass ceiling is not breaking anytime soon in nine out of ten companies that would benefit from women in business.

Theory Behind the Beginnings of the Boys and the Girls

The Economist reports: "Chris Clarke, the American-based CEO of Boyden, a firm of headhunters, and a visiting professor at Henley Management College in England, argues that women are superior to men at multitasking, team-building and communicating, which have become essential skills for running a twenty-first century corporation." So where did women lose ground? It all falls back to those early days of girls will be girls and boys will be boys ...

Today the business executive profile is: male, age 40-55, coming from middle America, or they could be Fred Trump's son, Donald Trump, or Nelson Rockefeller's son, or so many other 1960s executives' sons, the wealthy moguls of our American society. These 40-55-year-olds grew up when boys were boys and girls were girls. Therein lies the meat of the story:

The Boys

When boys were boys, they always wanted to be like dad! Little boys didn't cry, they bucked up and took the pain. They played ball, hung with the guys, and little girls were sissies and couldn't even throw a baseball from second base to first! This was the male bond. Little boys loved their mom, certainly moms deserved a hug, and they listened to mom when she called them for dinner. She helped with homework and made those great lunches. It wasn't cool to "listen to mommy." It wasn't cool to do what "mommy said" to do. The biggest fear for a little boy: "Don't be a mama's boy!"

Well, what an image for a male growing up. Dad was strong, the guys stuck together against those sissy girls and, worst case, don't be a mama's boy.

You can't possibly expect years of this programming tp leave a 40-55-year old male with the inclination to listen to a woman in business. Do you think they could possibly believe that a woman, with an impassioned argument about a financial subject, or, views contrary to the ideas of a less-than-stellar performing male peer, or a contribution about a major decision for the CEO, would be someone a male CEO should listen to?

No. Plain and simple the answer is no.

Do we expect that these little boys grew up to think independently? Of course, the mature approach would be to believe this. So how many male CEOs have female executive assistants to deal with their mom rather than call mom themselves?

The Girls

Now let's look at the little girls. When girls were girls, they were told to sit quietly and let their dad talk. They were told to speak softly, not to raise their voice. They worked hard to be "daddy's little girl." They spent a lot of time trying to make their dad proud of their accomplishments. Yet good grades, playing the piano and singing in the choir couldn't compete with their brother's home run in the last Little League game. Those little girls spent their time helping mom in the kitchen while the boys watched football with their dad's on Sunday afternoon. Smart girls went to college but the nudge of having a family tipped the ladder of success along the way.

Those little girls grew up, moved away from home, married and had children, and then went to work for the male 40-55-year old CEO. The mental replacement of pleasing dad with pleasing the CEO weighs heavy on the minds and emotions of the female working the glass ceiling. The feelings of inferiority rage deep within her psyche. How often do you fight back tears when making an impassioned argument against a decision that you know, with incredible business sense, is the wrong move altogether!

Wow, this is deep stuff! How can you possibly be the boss when you

"You'll go far in this firm, Ms Hobart - you think like a man."

live to please your dad? He is the boss transformed before you into the Senior Management team, one by one. Not even your male peers will give you confidence when you compete with them for the ear of the boss.

So we have now established the deepest reasons for this mess. Of course, we have the traditional reasons why women don't get ahead and why so many today just leave the corporate world to start their own business. Why fight the glass ceiling? Just make your own ceiling, which you control. (If you can't fight it then do it yourself!)

The National Foundation for Women Business Owners studied this subject in 2005 and found that women own approximately 7.7 million firms, an increase of 43% since 1990. Women are forming businesses at double the rate of their male counterparts. The men are sticking to the traditional companies like glue.

Men aren't going to change the GOOD OLD BOYS' NETWORK anytime soon. The jock talk and late-night boozing, golf outings and sales meetings outside the office are still the preferred methods of making things happen. The CEO controls the environment. One-on-one lunches and decisions over drinks are the outflow of the male "Boys Will Be Boys" behaviors. Women are uncomfortable in these environments and they should be. Respect for women in business won't come over drinks; it will come when the cocktails are replaced with meaningful work hours that accomplish much more than ever before. Let's see how women can understand their environment and move this picture to another paradigm…

Fast-Forward to the Motivations of Male Executives and Potential Female Executives

Fast-forward to today. Boys grow up and become the boss, CEO, CFO and COO of every major corporation in America. Girls grow up and work for the boss. What do they have to offer? Smart, fast-thinking, full of ideas, organized, a woman is still held back by her past, trying hard to please daddy, make him proud, don't ruffle the feathers or rock the boat. The images can make you dizzy. If you can't see straight, you can't articulate the message.

The First Steps Start With You!

- You must be happy with who you are. You know you are smart? Pretty? Well in whose eyes? You need to feel good, self-confident in your eyes first.
- Remember, it's not about you. It's about them. Insecure? Sure he is! He has something to prove too. He didn't get

the job because of his good looks or his connections or his being in the right place at the right time. Well, maybe he did and that makes him scared too.

Play on that—you are in control if you get into the FACT control mode:

1. No emotion
2. No crying
3. No laughing, no little girl squeaks
4. No weird clothes
5. No overly sexy clothes
6. Just the FACTS (remember the old TV show?) Just the FACTS

The Facts

FACTS are the most important TOOL TO SUCCESS! Did you hear what I said; did you read what I wrote? I'll say it again: FACTS are the most important TOOL TO SUCCESS.

The Presentation of the Facts

So your next question: What is the second most important tool? PRESENTATION of the FACTS is the second most important TOOL TO SUCCESS.

So what do we know? First, you must understand your end game. Your end game is what you want to accomplish, and why. You must know this in order to utilize strategy to get you there. So find it, present the facts to support it and, in the end, the result is that you will have all the answers. You hold all the cards and you will hold the promotion opportunity, the future role of your career, in your hands.

OK, lots of fancy talk. How do you do all this? Let's run a scenario that Jesse faced many times in her career. This happens in business across the country today:

Jesse worked for a CEO during her career. His name was John Miller. He made his money very young, using hustle and smarts. He bought and sold investments at the right time, and stepped up in his industry where luck is more often the answer than smarts. For John he was exceptional; he had both. He was sitting on a large corporation powder keg, waiting to take the company public when suddenly the market goes to pot! Now what? All the decisions of the past went south; the moves in the past wouldn't help get to the future. Jesse found herself in an amazing position. Now he would have to listen to her. Jesse's role was bigger than life; she could make financial recommendations that could save the day! Jesse's biggest challenge was to get John to listen to her. She had suffered from all the usual mistakes in the past. She had come from emotion, from innuendo, anger and frustration. No, those places wouldn't work, they never had. Jesse had to come from facts and the presentation of the facts; this was the key.

She created a matrix of alternatives, using her financial skills like she had never used them before. Jesse remained pleasant, but stilted, impassive and detached, presenting only the facts, without the emotion.

The result? John finally listened; he passed over all the good old boys, saw her words and numbers on the page, made the right decisions and today the company is public, successfully running the model Jesse created. If it remains on this path, it can continue to be successful. Could Jesse have become the CEO of that company? Maybe, but for her this was just a path to her real vision in life. She had a strong desire to be the CEO of her own opportunity. To be the CEO of her own shop and she did!

For you, the path awaits you; take the road to success, each step, by remembering the most important tools you possess. Do you remember what they are?

- FACTS—Facts are the most important tools to succeed.
- PRESENTATION—The presentation of the facts is the second most important tool.

At this point you should understand and be able to answer the question: "What Facts?" What facts are we talking about?

The facts depend on your area of expertise, but certain guidelines permeate every industry and every profession. FACTS are defined as a truth, a statement that cannot be challenged because its logic is based on truth and evidence, not opinion. FACTS cannot be challenged; therefore, if you can substantiate your advice, position or decision based on facts, you will face less of a challenge and make the focus the real reasons why your advice might not be followed.

OK, let's look at an example:

In order to evaluate an employee's performance you can say, "She works too slowly" or you can state a fact:

- ✔ Employee A processes 30 transactions per hour
- ✔ Employee B processes 10 of the same transactions per hour

The FACT that employee A does three times the work of employee B in the same one-hour period substantiates the statement "Employee B works too slowly." The fact emphasizes employee B's real productivity in the position, not the boss's opinion, the FACT.

Here's another example:

If we must choose between the boss's best friend who will charge the company $30.00 per hour to paint the offices, and another reputable company who will charge $20.00 per hour, the presentation of these facts remove emotion. You have done your job by getting fair and competitive bids for the job, and you can show how the company can save $10.00 per hour on that job while still getting good quality work. The answer cannot be presented more clearly; the boss must choose wisely!

Not every situation is as clear as these, so we have to remember that facts come to us in many ways:

- Use outside, expert, objective support
- Present to more than just the boss, solicit help from other management, both men and women
- Give the analysis time. Don't force it all at once
- Show alternative outcomes using the wrong answers and the right answers
- Cite previous examples of your good advice not taken. PRESENTATION is the key in this one—DO NOT SAY or imply "I TOLD YOU SO!"

All of this is meant to take the "Boys" and "Girls" emotionally out of the game completely. If you can't beat them on the golf course or in the bar, then beat them at the conference table!

"That's a very good suggestion, Miss Wilson - perhaps one of the men would like to make it?"

Word History

Ever have someone tell you a story and you are amazed at how articulate and descriptive they are? They paint a wonderful picture because of the words they use. Words can be the answer for or the downfall of every individual. With a woman, words tell the story of success or of failure. Let's examine the boys and girls theory in their word history.

When boys were young they could be boys and use fighting words, tough words, and those words would define the male character; tough, gritty, aggressive, determined, straightforward, smart, savvy. All those words said the "Boy" would be a great "Man" someday. If girls used the same words, they would hear: be polite, speak softly and act like a lady. Those same words meant one of two things for a girl; either she was a "bitch" already, or "butch," as in a tomboy, already. None of those words belonged in the description of a girl. OK, smart was allowed but was usually followed by nerdy or homely or brainy. Ever hear about those two girls walking down the street and someone saying, "Hey, there are Jesse and her big sister. You know, Jesse is the brainy one and her sister is the beauty." Only ladylike words are needed to describe the beauty and nerd-like words are needed to describe the brainy one.

Fast-forward to today. Where do these words take you in the business world of your future? Let's look at the following list of words and choose how you can Break the Glass Ceiling by using the Right Words to describe the men and women you work with and for, to help you stay on track.

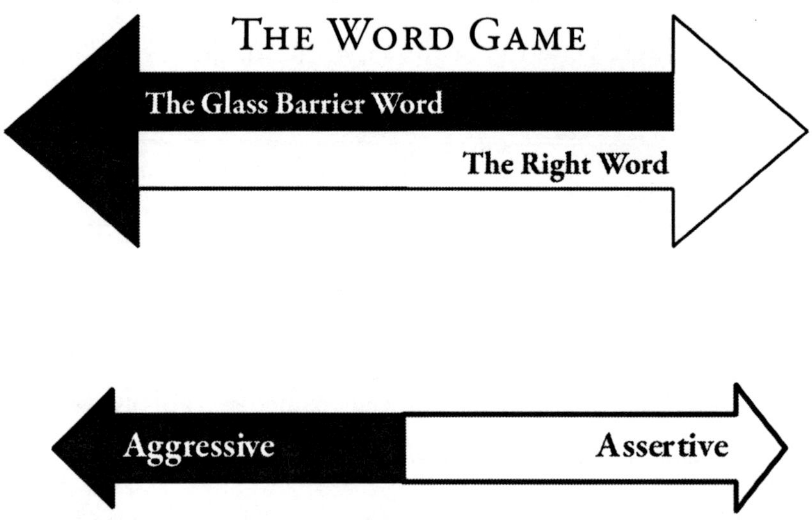

When women are **assertive**, they are seen as smart and sharp, not arrogant and pushy. Men can be **aggressive**, but if you challenge an aggressive male, you must push back with FACTS to keep from appearing jealous, emotional or catty in an effort to win points. Your fact-based position will win every time against the fast-talking, aggressive male counterpart.

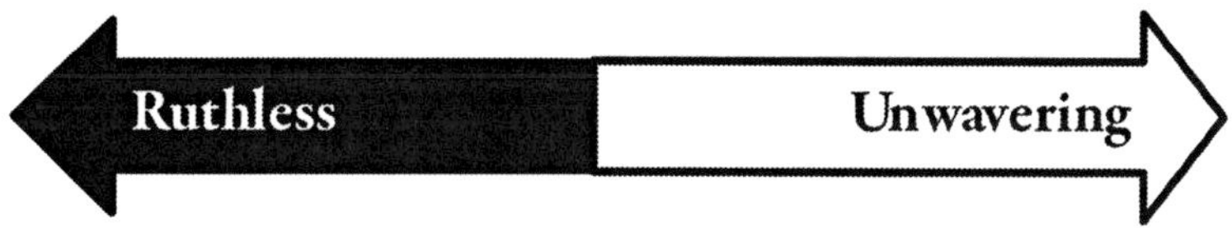

When women are **unwavering** in their message, it permeates everything they say and do. Again, the FACTS and lack of emotional response brings unwavering resolve to the top of its game. Don't confuse this with **ruthless** behavior. A lack of emotion married with ruthlessness means a cold fish! No one wants to work for that "B#@*#@". Men can be ruthless because they do it with a smile. Savvy oozes from them on the outside, while ruthless hides on the inside. Fight this battle with a smile; never engage in a toe-to-toe fight on this one because you will never win the slick war of words against a man who is savvy and ruthless. Actions, documented information and lots of patience are required here. Wait for the right time to step in and catch this guy. Letting him hang himself with his own rope is the only answer if your boss isn't able to see through his behavior. In the end, this is the most stress-free approach to the person, to the behavior and to your desire to come out on top.

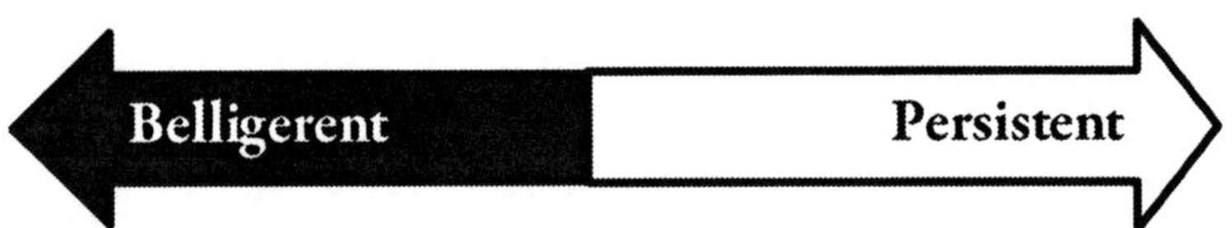

We have all experienced the guy in Operations who has it all, including great upward mobility. Why? He is **persistent** in his laser focus and follow-up. He stays on an issue until it happens the way he wants it to happen. Does execution ring a bell? Well, he makes the execution happen. He's forceful and sure of himself, no backing down; In Your Face works for him. Why don't you try that too? What are the results? Really bad news. Now everyone says you are **belligerent** and he is persistent. He is powerful and you are pushy. That didn't go well at all. We must realize that the mindset of those on the receiving end of this approach is different when it's delivered by a man. When men are In Your Face, they are proving their strength; they are supposed to perform this way. When a woman performs this way, the message is confused; women don't act this way. The In Your Face approach turns into the witch of the company flying around on her broom. Employees are heard to say, "Who does she think she is?" Jesse once lived through the Halloween season with a witch's broom parked outside her office door and a sign posted above the broom that read "CFO Parking." That's the message to an In-Your-Face woman. Jesse got it. The pushy approach led to the belligerent mindset, not the powerful, persistent, execution mindset.

To fix this problem you must use a softer tone, be less In Your Face.

Use more focused questions, follow up, set realistic deadlines with real dates to gain results. Stay on those items that are most important and show significant $$$ results for your company. Pick your battles and walk away from the rest. Don't discuss any of these with co-workers or subordinates. You will earn respect and move away from pushy to persistent in the value-added column.

Some smart, skilled, well-spoken men can step over the competition and be applauded for being a **fast tracker**. They will get the credit and no one will ever accuse them of "sleeping their way to the top." (Well, someday, you never know) or accuse them of being favored by the boss because of great cleavage or great legs or both! Why then can a smart, skilled, well-spoken woman face rejection by her peers and smirks from staffers when she steps over people and "**claws her way to the top**"? Because boys will be boys and girls will be girls. Go back to why men can't take orders from a woman without feeling like a mama's boy.

Jesse sat quietly as her boss gave a speech to the management team about good market conditions, bad market conditions and how those conditions dictated the ramping up of staff vs. staff reductions and layoffs. He talked about break-even points, fixed costs and variable costs. She was proud because she had discussed these concepts with the boss many times over the last few years, hoping that her information would prompt him to refuse to hire unnecessary positions and follow the costly ideas pushed by male counterparts. Jesse had spent much time talking about cost reduction measures and staying ahead of the curve. So, when she listened to his speech, she was amazed that he never mentioned learning these ideas from her, a woman or admitted that he had listened to a woman. He told his management team that he learned these ideas from an older man, a former CFO and business consultant.

Although Jesse knew that the business consultant did share this information as well as Jesse's point of view on the subject, she wasn't very happy. She was hurt that not one mention of her advice or counsel made it into the CEO's presentation. But, most importantly, she picked her battles carefully; Jesse understood that the CEO couldn't say he learned from a woman. A roomful of management would respect the advice of an older, experienced man over the advice from a younger woman. Jesse heard herself saying over and over, "Don't take it personally!" No emotion, choose your battles, pick your timing. Step over into successful positions anyway and get results because you believe you are a fast tracker. Your success comes from your smart, skilled, well-spoken attitude as much as your brain power.

I read somewhere that women trying to get ahead shouldn't giggle or act picky at lunch meetings. I disagree with that theory, although I like laughing much better than giggling; a giggle signifies a lack of confidence in your personality and presence. I strongly suggest confident, not cute, but cute has its moments-I know Jesse's very picky at lunches!

Where do you see yourself in this list? If you gave this list to your peers, your boss or your staff what would they say? How do you test out in your own eyes? Have you ever worked for a successful woman you hated? How many of these words do you attribute to your best female role model? Your worst? Take a few minutes and jot down a short biography of yourself. Look at which words you selected from this list to describe yourself on paper today. Now go back and write the biography you want for yourself tomorrow. Which words will you use?

The Right Words:

Heartless	Hard-nosed
Unfeeling	Businesslike
Stoic	Firm
Uncompromising	Focused
Inflexible	Thoughtful
Stubborn	Determined
Hard-lined	Strong
Destructive	Tear Down Barriers
Adamant	Unwavering
Slick	Smooth
Know-it-all	Experienced
Naïve	Open-minded
Full Of It	Self-confident
Dictator	Leader
Overbearing	Mentor

Words and Perception

Words alone won't always be your downfall. Man or woman, if your counterparts perceive your words differently from your intent, then the message is lost in perception. For Jesse, sitting in an executive team review and strategy session week in and week out, the distinction between the message and the perception of the message became very important. Just one of many examples of this issue played out in unnecessary drama. Here's how it went.

The COO, William, a very educated, experienced man well-respected in his field was tall, soft-spoken, yet serious about his role within the company. Jesse had much respect for this gentlemen overall, but this particular meeting day they faced some challenges.

"The sales-team received the list of potential distributors on Monday," said William. He made this statement in a proud voice, as this represented the completion of a request from the CEO, the follow-up and follow-through of the boss's request from the previous weekly meeting.

Jesse's mind immediately went to the rest of the story. Here it was Friday, a full five days since the list was given to the sales-team. "What happened? It's been five days since they got the list, do we know if they set any appointments?" Jesse asked.

William looked up. He seemed surprised by the question. "I don't know, why don't you ask them?" he said in a rather matter-of-fact way.

Jesse knew this was not going well. She immediately answered, "Ok," and wrote a note about the issue on her memo pad.

The meeting continued and the CEO, time and time again, came back to the focus on the distributors. This was crucial to the success of the company. The CEO expressed his concern that outside resources would be necessary for sales because clearly the sales-team did not and could not focus on these calls.

Jesse, in an effort to reinforce the message, chimed in, "A classic example of the team's lack of focus and follow-through is just what we discussed today. They know how important distributor calls are, yet the list of likely distributors they received from William on Monday hasn't even been addressed!"

William was furious. He perceived that Jesse was not questioning the management team's ability to perform but his ability to lead. Jesse's efforts to defuse the situation during the meeting were futile because the perception of Jesse's words far outweighed her intended message.

Hours later Jesse spoke to William in an effort to repair the damage. He explained how he perceived Jesse's message to be, 1. a lack of respect for his ability to manage the team, and 2. an effort to call him out in front of his peers. Jesse apologized again. Her intent had been neither, as her desire had been to reinforce the CEO's understanding that the team could not perform at the level required, not to disrespect William. This is an excellent example of words vs. perception.

In order to be sure your words are not misunderstood, you must assess the circumstances surrounding you prior to speaking. So learn from the lesson on the table:

- ✔ Who is your audience?
- ✔ Will your words be taken personally as an attack on character?
- ✔ Is your point necessary?
- ✔ Will it help the team (do something positive, not negative)?

Jesse's relationship with William went through many phases as they continued to work together. She learned his strengths, weaknesses, goals, and most importantly, his perceptions of her, her team, her role within the company, her words and her actions. The relationship evolved into one of mutual respect, but this took time. Any good working relationship will take time.

Every man and woman has personal objectives and perceptions that come with them from childhood into their careers. We need to take that into consideration when we speak, send e-mail or even just write a personal note.

So let's recap:

- Words are powerful tools you use to present the FACTS
- FACTS are the most important tool to your success
- Perception by the receiver of your words is almost as important as the words themselves
- Recognize the who, why and history of the receiver of those words to be sure they see and hear the message you send, the way you want it seen and heard.
- Remember, most of the time the issues are those of the receiver of information, not yours. When you put a magnifying glass on the issues with your words through FACTS, there is nowhere to run, the receiver of FACTS must face the truth of your message
- Be prepared to be supportive if your words create too much focus on the truth

Your best friend is your ability to be humble and compassionate so that relationship and respect can break the glass ceiling of perceptions. Women cannot earn the respect of a male executive without an overly sensitive understanding of the perceptions created throughout management history, our "boys" and "girls" history, our personal life experiences and our own insecurities. Don't take it personally; our interactions have more to do with our painted pictures of life than with what that clean canvas can do for tomorrow.

Step Three

Why Do Women Want to Break the Glass Ceiling Anyway?

What motivates today's woman to be more successful by society's standard of success?

Passion

Passion comes to different people in different ways because we are all wired differently. Jesse was wired with an overwhelming motivation summed up in a few words.

"Failure is not an option," Jesse would often say in interviews and meetings with life coaches or business coaches.

She lived and breathed this, not as words but as a way of life. So, when women have passion for raising a family, being a good cook, good homemaker, great soccer mom and PTA member, they have a clearer path to success, bring joy to others and love life. This is amazing to see and we can admire this in a woman. Jesse and many other women are wired differently; they're not sure why but its true. Throughout the ages, those women wired differently have taken many paths to their passion. From Joan of Arc to Eleanor Roosevelt, those women found a way to express their passion in their time.

Now, in today's world, we look at women like Margaret Thatcher and Princess Diana and see true-life passion as something great. We all can't be Margaret Thatcher but we can succeed in our own career and life by experiencing our passion with the "Dos and Don'ts" of our lives.

Dos and Don'ts

- We don't get there on the backs of others. Only when you surround yourself with good people, whom you acknowledge, does your leadership ability shine.

- Never take credit for ideas that belong to your team. Your ideas are yours and your ability to lead those with their own ideas is more important to your success than stealing ideas in an effort to look good.

- We don't shortcut! Know your material. *Cliff Notes* never got you more than a passing grade in school.

- Humility beats dictatorship every time. Later we will talk about how women who achieve power without a good foundation abuse the power and abuse the people they work with.

- Self-confidence can never be mistaken for arrogance, and arrogance will never breed self- confidence. Internal truth, your compass, will tell you the difference.

- Never leave the lesson on the table, but don't cry over spilled milk. People don't like being called out on a mistake. Speak in private and then find ways to prevent their mistake from recurring or affecting your future.

- As Steven Covey says, begin with the end in mind. All else is commercials during the movie! Every step taken is bringing you closer to your passion. You must consciously decide if each of these steps is necessary to achieve your result.

- Don't confuse looking at each step with measuring each step. The more you measure, the less you actually do. You can live your whole life getting ready to do instead of doing. Jack Canfield in *The Success Principles* talks about "Ready, Fire, Aim." This is a great principle because preparation for life allows your life to pass you by while you are busy preparing instead of living! So live, do it. Ready, fire, aim, then make corrections along the way and keep going. Use humility and passion as your compasses. Don't leave a carnage of bodies on the side of your road, but get on your road and start walking. Crawl first, if you have to, but start. Looking at the road only exercises your eyes, not your brain or your body!

Passion does not have to be a noun; in my book, it can be an action verb. It's the action of your life. Swing the hammer and break some glass so you can run, not walk toward the ladder of success.

Management Challenges for the Woman Working in a Man's World

When Women Are Insecure

Now that we have established the fact that it is still a "man's" world, what do we do? Although strides toward equality have come through the ranks, women in business continue to make several mistakes. Some have decided to become men instead of showing how women can compete and still be women. We can keep our female style and not turn into manhaters in order to succeed. Too many women think male-bashing is in vogue and shows how successful women conduct themselves today. That's not the answer. All male-bashing has done is emasculate the male population and create a bunch of overbearing females no one would ever want as their boss!

The overbearing female boss is ten times worse than an overbearing male boss. Why is that true? The overbearing male boss is that way due to business pressures and lack of management training. The overbearing female boss is that way because she usually has "something to prove." This makes her totally unfocused on business needs and way off on the potential strategic plan. This makes her the most difficult obstacle to the company's success. In many cases you can overcome her issues and make a successful transition for the company; in many cases it's a lost cause and time for you to move on.

For your career to succeed and your talent to be recognized, you need to continue the values and skills that got you interested in management to begin with. Moral and ethical behavior lead from quiet strength where you don't say many words, but the words you say have significant meaning and those around you will listen. Inroads into the "man's" world come in small steps and individual performance, not the MILLION WOMEN MARCH on Washington, D.C.

SCHWADRON
"WHAT YOU HAVE TO UNDERSTAND, MS. TITUS, IS YOUR GLASS CEILING IS MY GLASS FLOOR."

How Long Is too Long

How much time should you give an opportunity before you push for more or move on? Let's examine a sample opportunity:

Jesse felt great! She had snagged that super executive financial position and she felt like a star female performer. What next? The first few days were very scary. All eyes were watching her. At least she felt like that. She had a whole new financial team looking to her to hit the ground running and know the background of every problem they were already facing, plus new ones creeping out of the woodwork. Wow, it was tiring just thinking about it. Although Jesse considered herself a very talented financial executive, she knew better than to think she was Superwoman. Jesse was also aware that she was probably the only one expecting that of her. If she didn't, she wouldn't have risen through the ranks quickly, moving from position to position and achieving the FAST TRACK results that her peers were drooling over. Jesse took a deep breath and used all the skills she worked so hard to master. What was on that list? You have heard them all before; the TO DO list, The Mission Statement, List of Goals and Objectives and your Personal Business Plan. Ok, maybe this was a little heady to start with, so her first move was to absorb as much about that company as she could as fast as she could and dig in.

Before she could blink, four years had gone by and she began to feel like a part of the furniture. Her ideas were good but the CEO was starting to look to others for answers. How could that happen? Presentation, focus on the facts? Jesse had to face the reality that the CEO didn't want to face reality. She identified the good, the bad and the ugly, and had gotten so tired of putting up with a lack of cooperation that she had basically become too tired to put forth a fight for support for her version of the business plan. Jesse was at an impasse. Her choices were, a) find new resolve to move her message closer to acceptance by the CEO, or b) accept that it was time to move on to the next challenge in her career. She began to look for that next opportunity that would increase her income, move her closer to her objective and challenge her on her road to success.

Jesse had decided it was time to move on in her career. This accomplished two things, 1. gave her a fresh chance to enhance her career, and 2. gave the company she was currently working for an opportunity for fresh blood, new ideas and energy to get the job done.

How many times have you read a business magazine where the executives of one company have resigned for personal reasons, only to see, two articles later, that one of them has replaced the executive of another major company? One thing lacking in those articles is the number of women filling those shoes. Once again, that GLASS CEILING is there, unspoken and ever present.

The Challenge of Success

By now you are probably saying to yourself "Doesn't she realize many of us are CEOs, CFOs and COOs? We have seen many examples of very successful women." I hear you! The problem, once "success" is achieved, is the propensity to throw it all away can get in the way of doing something great. That's not to say that men in this same position don't do the same, but women can't afford mistakes. It's too costly. The magnifying glass is focused on women executive failures as a measure of whether women can handle the job.

The simple message that rings true for all of us is that your personal success must be based on a deep understanding that you earned that success; you deserve that success, and others achievements of similar or higher levels of success should not and will not interfere with your success. There is such a thing as scarcity mentality. When we are children, we believe that if you want a toy that your friend is holding then you must be the loser and they are the winner. The fact that you can be just as happy or happier with a different toy, copy of that toy or a better toy doesn't cross a child's mind. They haven't learned that yet. As parents we try to teach abundance mentality to our children.

Women in business also have a very hard time with abundance mentality. Praise for you takes away from me. Not true. Women with confidence and smarts who are armed with FACTS and the proper presentation of the facts, walk with a certain air about them. They are never fazed by others who achieve success.

Jesse's past experiences played a role in creating obstacles to her ability to achieve success. At 30 she saw the opportunity to grab the brass ring. The coveted CFO title was clearly one she deserved, earned and thought she would receive after she spearheaded the company's IPO in the late 1980s. Yes, 30 was young, but not for an aspiring male at that time. Jesse's boss, the CEO, could not bring himself to take the chance. He hired a male CFO he had worked with before. Jesse was devastated. How could he do this? Her role would remain as it was, with the odd title of Director of Profit Planning and Investor Relations. Who had ever heard of that? The good news was Jesse didn't give up. Cooperating with the CFO was a difficult challenge, and she tried to look forward to advance her role in the future. By the time change of ownership was on the horizon, the CEO admitted he was mistaken and should have given Jesse the title and the job of CFO. Too bad this all happened after he and Jesse had moved on to other companies. A look back creates a better view of the future. Jesse never forgot that her best approach to adversity was to work at her best in the role she was in and not pine over the role she didn't get.

From the National Association for Female Executives, to *Career Journal*, to female-executive coaching companies, an entire industry has arisen to help women avoid the pitfalls of success. Since there are too many to remember, I suggest you browse the Internet under Executive Women to find your mentor, coach or classes to assist in this area.

Society has given us several examples of successful women who have thrown away success. One of the classic examples is the well-touted achievement of Hewlett Packard (HP) in their ability to bring women to the role of CEO. First Carly Fionia held the role of CEO and spent her time with HP trying to merge the computer giant with Compaq Computers. As one of just eight female CEOs at the Fortune 1000 companies just a few years ago, her failure to pull off the merger and grow the company was under Wall Street's magnifying glass. Her replacement, Patricia Dunn, who was, in fact, part of the group pressing for Fionia's removal, had failures of her own, including a very public scandal regarding the culprit leaking news from inside the company to the press.

Many articles have been written in the last few years about these two women. I am sure other famous failures, such as those related to ENRON executives, WorldCom and Tyco, focused on the CEOs approach to their company's success, but few of these articles focused on the fact that a woman was at the helm and was she ready, capable or just picked for her good looks. Have you read any articles that say the CEO of ENRON was picked for his good looks?

Until women make significant inroads into all top positions, the questions will continue and we must be ready with the right answers.

The Man/Woman Dynamic: Don't Fall Into the Trap

Since the beginning of time the man/woman dynamic has impacted society. From Adam and Eve to Cleopatra and Marc Antony, to Romeo and Juliet, to George and Martha and, yes, even to Bill and Hillary, the man/woman dynamic has changed history. As boys and girls we learn the rules of dating, marriage and, now alternative lifestyles. Has anyone really taught men and women how to behave in the boardroom, or executive office, during a business lunch or, no less, the business dinner? What about when the President of the United States' most trusted advisor is a woman who is not his wife? Should they have private meetings or dine alone together? (Don't tell me the president is never alone. Bill Clinton proved that's not true.) The man/woman dynamic has twists and turns that society, psychology and political pundits have yet to fully comprehend.

Blocking the career path of women today stands three levels of interaction: 1) The Male Boss; 2) The Male Peer; and 3) the Male Staffer. Each of these man/woman dynamic interactions holds their distinct challenges and obstacles, as well as, the proper approaches to help you unblock the path.

I hope, by understanding where you are, you can apply the right stuff to each, and earn a rung on the ladder to success along the way.

Now lets tear apart each of the three relationships and see what we can learn from experience.

#3 The Staffer

As Jesse found herself in positions of authority, the mix of staff working for her always included both male and female employees. Having two sons of her own, she always looked at the younger male staff as her children. Not necessarily a good thing. It was always best to remember she was the boss, not their mom, and work from that premise. Occasionally included in the mix of staff was the older male staffer who possessed some business experience. Jesse turned a blind eye to the man/woman dynamic except to always apply three basic rules:

- No private lunches with the male staff. Jesse tried to take staff to lunch as a group so she could never be accused of showing favoritism or partiality.
- No attending business parties without her spouse.
- No private, behind-closed-door meetings with male staff.

Beyond those three basic rules she felt pretty confident in her overall approach. After all, Jesse, as a mentor, had much to offer her team. One should never underestimate the man/woman dynamic! While Jesse's intent was to mentor, and she thought her attentions were evenly distributed among her team, the older male staffer took her attention personally and eventually began to express his appreciation with innuendo and overt comments. Jesse found herself caught off guard and playing defense. She immediately faced the issue head-on with clear, concise words, to eliminate any possible misunderstanding from that point forward. Her mentoring approach immediately took a different path, and she became keenly aware that the man/woman dynamic can be huge in the relationship between female boss and male staff. MENTAL NOTE: Add this to the list of dos and don'ts:

- Do training sessions in groups
- Identify fast trackers and use Human Resource team-supervised performance reviews to provide tools for the individual to improve their skills.

#2 The Peer

Another difficult dynamic occurs when a woman is a member of an executive management team. Jesse's early career included a role as part of a 12-person executive management team. Her job title did not denote a position that could be considered as senior as some of the other members of the team. Her age, early 30s made some of those men nervous. When Jesse spoke, giving her expert opinion on a topic, several of the male team members would threw out jabs of innuendo, almost to the point of sexual harassment. The old school CEO allowed this to happen; well it was the early 80s and you could say he didn't know better. This approach promoted the good old boys' network. Talk about trial by fire! Jesse worked hard to abide by those all-important rules of the man/woman dynamic and, with THE PEER the rules were gospel:

- No private lunches with male peers. In circumstances where she was working with a male peer on a project, she would hold all meetings in the office during office hours. When possible, maintain group activity, including lunch.
- No business parties without your spouse. This includes drinks after the management workshop event. You may think that if you are not at these events your male counterpart will get the beat on you, make progress, and be Johnny-on-the-spot with the boss. Don't do it! Positioning will come from your smarts, not drinks at the bar.
- No private meetings behind closed doors. Too many images of the man/woman dynamic of misunderstanding intent can occur when long periods of time are spent together behind closed doors.

#1 The Boss

The man/woman dynamic most analyzed is the male CEO who has, at his right hand, the female corporate executive. Every management book in the world will encourage the CEO to keep his team at his side. Important meetings, out-of-town events, key negotiations, all of these events require

"I didn't get the promotion. The interviews took place in the mens' room."

the counsel of the most trusted advisor. This causes significant concern and can be pointed to as a significant cause of women facing large glass ceilings today. Not only does the CEO now have to listen to a woman, but the female in the role of CFO or COO has to be ten times better than her male counterpart, and perfect in delivering the message to prevent the CEO from feeling the effects of the "Mama's Boy" syndrome.

How inappropriate does it appear when the CEO and CFO are male and female and are traveling together? This doesn't even need to be on the same plane, just to the same event. Time together without their spouses can appear to be inappropriate. So, if you have to choose between a female executive as your right hand, or a male good old boy, what would you do? If the Board of Directors had to choose between hiring a new CEO from internal resources, the excellent female candidate or a dynamic male candidate who, just by the nature of the beast, has already had experience as a CEO of a smaller organization, you know the decision—the GUY!

Women Face Choices

The boards of today's major corporations are predominately male. The desire of corporate America to keep the status quo promotes the "don't rock the boat" approach. To maintain a low, non-scandalous profile, those boards will continue to make the same decision time after time. This is not meant to scare away all prospective women executives. However, many women are successfully making the choice to walk away from the traditional corporate environment and start their own company.

For those who choose to stay and fight it out, your timetable may run slightly different than most of your male counterparts.

As Jesse found in 26 years of corporate experience, it was not at age 30, 35 or 40 that she reached the pinnacle of corporate success. It wasn't until age 45 that her role as CFO had true meaning in corporate America. Her positions framed themselves around those important family years. Early in her career, before her children were born, she drove full force into corporate America. Once, while taking a company public and representing the voice of the company she spent every meeting break in the restroom while morning sickness ruled the day. Her meals consisted of ice chips!

When the boys appeared on the scene (by the way, she actually stopped working long enough to deliver the children), her outlook changed. Family now filled her time and energy, and business was a distant second. Although, looking back Jesse would have preferred to take a real leave of absence from work to raise her family, she did take positions that allowed for a more flexible schedule. Once her boys were older and more independent and responsible, (you need both, by the way, to give them more freedoms - that's a different book!), Jesse again focused on finding positions that were more challenging as a CFO. Her reputation as one of the top CFOs in her particular industry was a tribute to her desire to give her best as a woman in a man's world.

Those of you who want to improve your ability to manage the man/woman dynamic, especially as a major executive in the role of COO, CFO, vice president in manufacturing or marketing, or any position working closely with a male CEO, should apply the basic rules we have discussed, plus a few more. Putting it all together, it looks like this:

- No private lunches: sometimes this cannot be prevented. If that happens:
    - ✔ Make sure it's necessary.
    - ✔ Have a meeting agenda
    - ✔ Sit opposite, not beside the boss
    - ✔ Keep personal conversation to a minimum. Of course, caring people know about your family, but never share marital highs or lows with the boss. Remember, he is not your counselor; he is the man who needs to take counsel from you!
    - ✔ Do not allow your CEO to share his marital issues with you. You are his business advisor; stay on task, stay focused, stay professional

- ✔ No business parties without your spouse. If you find yourself at a group event, conference or seminar where you will be socializing, use the golden rule—no alcohol. It's important to keep 100% in control, and alcohol will only blur your ability to remain socially polite but always professional. Stay with the group at all times. Do not leave with your boss unless it's in a group. Even the most innocent of events can be perceived to be less than innocent.

- No private meetings behind closed doors. Again, very difficult in some cases where you want to avoid the distractions of hallway traffic. In that case keep the length of the meeting to a minimum. Be sure to have an agenda and begin and end on time. The effects of the private meeting can be positively influenced by your behavior in all other situations.

The three basic rules need to be combined with your consummate presentation of exceptional knowledge, execution and presence in the company. How well you perform in your primary functions of executive management, be it finance, operations or marketing, dictate your ability to break the glass of gender discrimination with your staff, your peers, your boss and that decision making board of directors. Do your job well so your job will be noticed and help your career.

Back to Boys and Girls

Your personal appearance is also quite important. I know I am politically incorrect to discuss this but someone has to.

How many of you remember the boys being praised for getting dirty? Whether from football practice or sliding into third, mom and dad were always proud of the boys who got dirty in the course of becoming a man. How many remember mom worrying that her son didn't eat enough? "Don't worry," she would say, "he'll run it off working up a sweat." Girls, did you get that same message? No. Dirty was a bad thing. "You'll ruin your new clothes or get hurt," mom would say. "Don't run around. And, "Girls shouldn't eat too much, you know. You need to watch your looks.". Sound familiar? Some moms were so overbearing that their daughters suffered from eating disorders.

Fast-forward to adults. More men today are watching their looks, but corporate America is still riddled with men who are in less than the best condition. Ladies, not so for you. At age 48, you must look like age 35. At age 55, you must look like age 42, so age 40 is the new 30, and so on.

Please don't buy into the belief that looking smart and professional means no makeup, loose fitting clothes, and natural hair that's turning grey in several spots on your head! You are injuring to your chances for getting ahead.

The smart professional woman combines caring for herself, (exercise, eating right, weight control, professional clothing, hairstyle, hair color and makeup), with her verbal and written communication skills. Remember, a picture is worth a thousand words. They SEE you before they HEAR you. Make it count.

- No unnecessary weight: You will be less tired, less prone to illness; and, your brain works better on healthy food rather than junk food.

- No overtly sexy clothes: You are a professional in business, not in the world's oldest profession. Everyone knows you have a nice figure, including those eye-catching parts! There is nothing worse than speaking with a man who is talking to your chest instead of to you.

- No strange hair color: This includes natural gray. If you want to remind a male about taking orders from mom, then show your gray. No matter what age you are, gray is not flattering.

- No Earth Child attire: You have a figure and, unless you work for Greenpeace, your figure can be professionally clothed in shapely, fashionable attire, not boxy, boring or baggy!

- High-Heel shoes are good for your feet. This may not be a true statement, but most good business shoes do have a nice heel. Don't shy away from a good-looking shoe because you want comfort. Nice shoes complete the outfit.

- Always dress one step better than your staff. If the dress code says no stockings, wear them anyway. If the dress code says jeans on casual day, wear only dress jeans accompanied by a fashionable business shirt and jacket. If the dress code says slacks for women, always go with a pantsuit.

- Looking good helps you feel good. Feeling good helps your self-confidence in all interactions with your business environment.

Step Four

Management Strategies Everyone Should Know

Even women executives could use some pointers on management strategies that appear necessary to a company's success, yet very few companies can claim success in the implementation of these strategies and concepts. Jim Collins and Jerry Porras examined this concept in both Jim's *Good to Great* and Jim and Jerry's *Built to Last.* Many years of research on the best, most successful companies in our history provided the authors with unique insight into those strategies and concepts that led to and were ever present in all of these successful companies. I strongly suggest reading this material; better yet, listen to the cds and you will receive not only good solid information but the passionate delivery of the authors who believe strongly in their message.

Here are just a few concepts which were part of the life experiences that Jesse felt were an integral part of her success.

Strategic Planning

Strategic planning is a concept buzzword that has been used and abused by most management training programs. The problem with this concept is that most can teach about it, but very few have ever experienced the day-to-day confusion of business which rules how well strategic planning is utilized.

The management of a company can easily create a strategic plan, but implementation skills are where most managers are weak. Managers are untrained in most management concepts needed to follow through on the implementation of strategic concepts. For example, let's say your company has a department which provides a service in support of the main product line, such as hotel housekeeping. The hotel's strategic plan may say let's market to this traveler at these certain rates: let's use direct mail and Internet advertising portals to let the traveler find our hotel and book reservations. Once the traveler makes a reservation and arrives for their stay, housekeeping becomes critical. If the rooms are not ready in a timely fashion, your customer must wait for check-in. If they are given the room and housekeeping has done a poor job of preparing the room, the customer will be upset and find it unacceptable. The hotel must then transfer them to another room that is prepared properly. This will affect the hotel's occupancy rate. Let's say housekeeping does a poor job of timing their room cleaning, then the customer spends the day being a tourist only to come back to a dirty room. This is very upsetting to a customer. The housekeeping department certainly doesn't participate in the strategic planning for the marketing of the hotel, but housekeeping is an integral part of the success of the strategic plan. If the management of that hotel doesn't properly manage the housekeeping department, a strategic plan is a waste of time.

If your managers have the basics, the fundamentals to make sure that the housekeeping department is efficient and effective, they can utilize all of management's talents to create that strategic plan, implement the plan, measure the results and take positive action every day to ensure the plan's success.

Who participates in the strategic plan?

Although upper management may set the overall goal of any company such as "TO MAKE MONEY," it would be appropriate for the company to have a loftier goal, a Mission Statement that incorporates the goals of ownership (to make money) and the other goals of a good quality organization, such as:

- ✔ provide quality products
- ✔ good customer service
- ✔ job satisfaction for its employees

The way to develop this Mission Statement is to ask all members of the company to participate in the endeavor. Ask the opinion of the porter as well as the programmer, the secretary as well as the vice president. Once everyone participates and agrees on the Mission Statement, the Corporate Goals and Objectives, which help achieve the Mission Statement, can be formed and give birth to the Strategic Plan. If all participate in the development of the Strategic Plan, then all have a stake in its success. This happens when everyone participates in the implementation of the plan as well as the measurements of its success.

Several books have been written on Strategic Planning. I highly recommend: *Simplified Strategic Planning: A No-Nonsense Guide for Busy People Who Want Results Fast!* by Robert W. Bradford, J. Peter Duncan, Peter Duncan, Brian Tarcy

Meetings vs. Analysis

Where should you spend your time once the Strategic Plan is developed? Should you spend your time meeting with departments? Should you spend your time analyzing all the data created on a daily basis? The answer is yes.

The real key is when and how much of each is effective in running your business.

When management spends all of its time meeting with each other, you get meeting overkill. The results: a) a lack of employee communication, and b) manager burnout.

When management spends all of its time analyzing data you get overkill. The results: a) loss of business perspective, and b) information overload.

When management can balance the need for meetings with the need for analysis, then you will have effective use of management's time. Once a Strategic Plan is created, you should create a set of daily, weekly and monthly reports, which measure the results of the plan. Management should meet with specific department heads on an individual basis to review results and make those small corrective moves that keep that department on course. Management should also bring the team together so that every member is aware of the policies and progress made by the company toward results.

Analysis of data takes many forms. Trends tend to be the most informative tool that a company can use. The trend over the last six months, the trend year over year, the trend created by understanding seasonality, all help in understanding where your company stands today and what you can expect in the future. If you are a car dealer and the four weeks after tax season have shown a positive spike in car sales, year after year, then this year be prepared to take full advantage of that spike. Run your most strategic advertising campaign so you have maximum exposure prior to and during that peak period. In doing so your company will not only be more successful during that period, but your success will be incrementally greater than what you might have achieved had you maintained the same level of exposure you have the rest of the year.

Trends can also show you signs of deterioration in areas of your business. You can tell if costs are growing steadily in one area while productivity is slowing in a companion department. This could be an early indicator of failures in internal control, failures in department management, effects of changes in personnel, and so on. By analyzing this data in a timely manner you can stop the bleeding sooner rather than later.

Be careful not to overanalyze the data available. Be selective and stick to the major numbers. This will keep you from burying yourself in detail. As they say, you need to be able to see the forest amongst the trees.

THE SNAPSHOT—this is called many different things by many different advisors. I call it the snapshot. It represents those Five Key Indicators in your particular business that management needs to know everyday in order to give the team the right daily plan for the company. Put those Five Key Indicators on one piece of paper. It doesn't have to be pretty—it has to be effective...

Effectiveness vs. Efficiency —Can They Work Together

We see so many management courses concentrate on the efficiency of an operation. Getting more paper processed faster makes us more efficient.

The big question should be "How effective are we?"

The marriage of efficiency and effectiveness is a mystery to most, even those working in the management training area. There are several factors which act as catalysts or are integral parts of the strategy of efficiency vs. effectiveness.

First and foremost, we must remember that we are working with people, not machines. The machines we use today are still run by people, programmed by people, maintained by people, invented by people. The human nature factor plays a big role in the effectiveness of our crew. Once you factor in human nature you will begin to formulate a plan, person-by-person, and function-by-function. You can now make the most of your efforts for efficiency, which makes a happy marriage with your staff's ability to be effective in their job performance.

The human nature factor plays an important role in the corporate culture of your departments. For example, let's say your owner/manager has a knee- jerk reaction to daily events; somehow it feels like they spend most of their time fighting corporate fires around the office/business. This projects a corporate culture of a frantic work environment with no structure, rhyme or reason to the daily activities. In this environment no one is really sure what the long-term priorities are; goals and objectives may not change, but strategy to achieve those goals and objectives change on a daily, maybe hourly, basis. In this case, it's best to move away from that owner/manager because a leopard doesn't change its spots. Unless you are very good at counterculture, you don't stand a chance of making progress in this environment.

If you are lucky enough to make strides in a counterculture environment, you should emphasize a sense of calm amongst the staff. Work with your staff on creating a set of goals and objectives, a main long-term strategy to accomplish those goals, and a daily set of priorities to accomplish those goals. One can never eliminate all firefighting, but if you bring a sense of calm to the crew, they will have a better chance of managing those fires efficiently and effectively. By doing this, even the firefighting will be in line with the long-term strategy to accomplish your goals and objectives.

The other important factors in effectiveness-married-to-efficiency are the mechanics of the jobs. The technology factor plays a key role in your department's ability to do its job. Advances in technology must be thought out in order to blend those advances with the already functioning operations of your departments. A person working in the same job for more than six months has developed his or her own work patterns; if you implement changes due to advances in technology, you must find a way to blend those advances with that person's developed work patterns. The disruptions which can occur if you do not plan this process well are significant. More important than the change in technology is the person's attitude toward the change. Even the best advances will cause disruption in the work pattern and could cause attitude problems. Patience with your staff reigns king when dealing with these changes and attitudes. Remember, the staff person is the same efficient, effective employee you have relied on for the last year. Remember that they are going through a major disruption in their work pattern and the attitude you are getting is not directed at you, but at the change itself. Multiply this problem by the number of employees involved in this technology change and you will find yourself overwhelmed. Step back, set yourself a plan to work with each member of your department to ease the fears created by this new technology, LISTEN to your workers so they know you feel their pain, that you understand why this new technology is giving them trouble, and that you will work with them to SOLVE THE PROBLEM. Those actions alone will help to ease the attitude problem. Without an attitude problem, together, you can tackle the logistics of making the new technology work for them and for the company.

The staffing factor is another piece of the efficiency vs. effectiveness puzzle. How do you know when you are overstaffed? Understaffed? Does this question only arise when you are behind in your work, or when the company is losing money? The answer is yes, but these questions should come up during your strategy sessions, during the development of the plans to accomplish your long-term goals and objectives, as well as your daily priorities. Important—do not share your concerns with your staff. Sounds like simple common sense, but office politics often affect management in such a way that you might express your concerns to a member of your staff that you consider your confidante or to another manager. By expressing your concerns to those persons, you expose your staff to possible and unnecessary stress about job security.

So you go it alone, you analyze the data and make your decisions. Good, bad or indifferent, you make those decisions. There is nothing worse than lack of decisiveness when it comes to people and their jobs.

Management Values Everyone Should Know

Once you incorporate strategic concepts into your everyday management profile, you need to look inside to be sure that you have the core values necessary to bring humility and passion to your career. Here are some of the values that Jesse struggled with while working her way to the top.

Loyalty—A Corporate Benefit or Not?

Companies begin their existences with a few good people, a few good ideas. Over time loyalties to individuals, employees, vendors and ideas take shape. Some may consider this an important part of their corporate culture. Some may rely so heavily on loyalty that it impedes all other forms of progress.

When do you abandon loyalty as your measure of performance for employees? Theory has it that loyalty should never be a measurement of performance for any employee, vendor or idea.

Employees need guidelines, rules, goals and discipline.

A well-written job description and list of performance measurements will not only create a good productive employee but, at no extra cost, loyalty. Be loyal to those performance measures when evaluating an employee and you will never have to keep an employee who does not perform, but is loyal to you. In reality, by not performing at their best, they are being disloyal and abusing your confidence in them.

When do you abandon loyalty as your measure of a vendors' performance? How closely do you build that working relationship with your business partners, the banks, insurance companies, product brokers and suppliers? Theory says that these relationships walk a fine line between necessary and detrimental.

The first step to the successful understanding of loyalty vs. good business practices takes place in the purchasing department. A strong set of guidelines and a purchasing agent that understands the three-bid standard will keep all your vendors providing the company with the best price every time.

Vendors are notorious for winning an account, catering to those employees in the company that can help them keep the account, and then slowly adjusting their pricing to make the most of each business transaction. In each of these cases, when the purchasing agent remains loyal to the three bid process, vendors can never become so ingratiated with company employees that price and service to the company suffers.

As a corporate executive, you must be ready to put the company first. Business relationships develop over time, and sometimes they outweigh what is best for the company. Every bank, insurance company, broker, merchant processor and supplier will again have opportunities to win the account, hopefully, at a better price and with better service in the future.

You shouldn't be afraid of change, but remember, don't burn your bridges; yesterday's business partner is tomorrow's contact for the future.

Ethics—A Corporate Necessity?

In today's environment Ethics is a very scary word, overused and overabused. True ethical behavior has become dependent on who you are and whether your definition of ethical behavior fits the moment. But the reality of human nature is that true ethics must shine through for our society today to survive.

For business to be successful, it must be built on true ethical behavior, or today's successes will be followed by tomorrow's very public failures. The parade of companies in the news, such as ENRON, Global Crossing, WorldCom, Arthur Anderson, Xerox and smaller, less well-known companies, have crossed the paths of many of our corporate executives today. They have experienced the boom of success, the pressure to perform and the inherent failure when management decides that they can cut corners to make that success happen.

Jesse's experience came in the early 80s, when she worked for a company whose desire to succeed outweighed their ability to perform. In that case, questionable accounting methods for capitalizing emerging software, research and development costs could not rescue a failing business plan model. Jesse recalled one CEO in her past, when questioned about the validity of a transaction, told her, "Take my word for it, you're not an auditor anymore."

Jesse's next move? Find another job!

One thing unethical behavior cannot mask is lack of business profits, which leads to lack of cash flow. Ever hear the expression "Cash Is King"? Ask any financial person in business and they will tell you that this statement is very true. Unless your lack of ethics includes robbing a bank or kiting funds, then your lack of cash flow will eventually eat you alive!

So how do you go through life holding your head up high and maintaining the ethics necessary to fulfill your personal goals and objectives without leaving every job in a hurry? It's a blending of timing issues. First and foremost, you, as a member of executive management, must not get caught up in the frenzy to make the numbers look good. Secondly, you must decide whether your advice, counsel and impact are enough to turn around a potentially bad situation. Work toward those goals, and when you find the brick wall that says, "Do it my way, not the right way," then you begin your search for your next management assignment in another company. You must be a realist and know when to throw in the towel. Don't take it personally; remember, your goals and objectives belong to you and your career, not the company you work for today. That company may be long gone while you are still working to achieve your ultimate career success. Never sell yourself short on ethics. Once they are gone, they are very hard to get back...

Praise and Recognition—Valuable to Retention?

Ever hear the expression "Praise in public and discipline in private"? Someone very wise said this once and it stuck. I don't know who that person was or I would give them credit for it. Just take my word for it; I didn't think this one up myself. There is nothing more vital to human nature than one's desire to look good in front of others. The boss, who didn't get to be the boss because he or she graduated first in their class at boss school, doesn't always recognize that people are at the core of success for his/her business. That means they don't get this concept very well. Usually they yell first and praise during two minutes in their office after the big blowout in public. This is backwards and does nothing to instill respect for that CEO; nor does it create commitment by the team, another required management value. There is nothing like office/workplace gossip to get employees off track. If they have lots of gossip about the boss's last blowup with the day shift supervisor, they will spend every spare moment talking amongst themselves and very little productive time getting work done. It's so hard not to participate in idle gossip around the office. Handle this carefully and make a shiny plaque that says "PRAISE IN PUBLIC AND DISCIPLINE IN PRIVATE" and hang it in the CEOs office.

That might be a little unrealistic. So a more subtle approach is:

- Practice what you preach and treat all of your own employees with respect, as you praise in public and discipline in private.

- Use your counseling position with the boss to explain the concept and cite examples where the opposite has happened under their watch and the results were detrimental to the success of the company.

- Work with the human resources department, (or designated HR person for a small company), to come up with incentive programs that publicly reward employees for their successes.

- Use documented write-ups to discipline inappropriate work performance and behavior. This will improve morale as well as properly document issues with employees for their personnel file and help prevent potential exposure to worker issues such as EEOC violations, wrongful termination or unemployment claims.

If you take the lead in this area of employee relations you can easily show almost instant results in creating a positive culture and attitude among the staff. You may be responsible for a companywide turnaround that could impact the financial future of the organization. Employees who are happy with their work environment perform better and interact better with customers than those who are disgruntled. This attitude adjustment impacts turnover and productivity in a positive way and could, in the long run, save the company much needed payroll dollars. Who wouldn't want to save money and have happy employees?

Leadership vs. Taking Orders

When Jesse was a child, her father and mother used to say, "Be a leader, not a follower." Good advice for a child. If your friends were breaking the rules, should you follow them to be cool and part of the crowd, or should you be a leader and break away from the crowd to follow the right path? Well, these values work in business just the way they did when our parent were guiding us as children. There is only one difference; sometimes you must take orders in order to be a leader.

That doesn't seem to jive, does it? If you take orders then how can you be a leader? Does a leader take orders from others? Good questions. We can try to answer all of them without getting so confused we have to erase this paragraph and start over.

Think of leadership qualities as a state of mind, not a position in life.

Think of leadership qualities as decisions you make for yourself. Will I be one of the crowd or will I stand out amongst my peers?

Think of leadership as a concept you can implement as a manager or you can shy away from in your management style. Women must grasp the concepts of leadership at a much faster pace than their male counterparts. You don't have time to waste.

A leader is someone who thinks outside the box, who is not afraid to say what's really going on within the organization, and who stands by those issues by going back to our two basic important rules: the facts and the presentation of the facts which support the position stated. These facts will not be disputed in the way opinions can. These facts must be accompanied by ideas and plans for implementation of those ideas which will improve on the current situation by, a) changing it completely, b) reinforcing the current position to see it to its intended results, or c) reversing a previous position because, frankly, the plan just didn't work!

In many cases, once you have agreed to the CEO's plan, whether you think it can work or not, you must follow orders and implement the plan. By following orders and implementing the CEO's plan, you may gather facts and figures which support the plan or refute the plan. In either case, you need to follow orders so that your next move to show results will be treated with the level of respect that a leader deserves. If you whine and complain throughout your implementation of the CEO's plan, YOU might be seen as the cause of the plan's failure.

Leadership skills are some of the hardest skills and values to develop and nourish. By utilizing Leadership Skills you can:

- Increase your ability to remove emotion from the work environment which will assist you in implementing plans you don't agree with

- Work with other managers you don't like or believe in

- Avoid office talk about the CEO, which undermines any positive implementation of a good or potentially good CEO endorsed plan

A leader keeps frustrations to themselves. Never share frustrations with employees who work for you, or employees who work for another department and definitely never share frustrations with other managers and peers.

As a matter of practice,
never share frustrations with ANYONE!

A leader does their homework. (This is for both male and female managers, in case there are male mangers smart enough to read this book and gain insight into management from another perspective,) Know your stuff. If you are fully informed on every aspect of a situation, you, with your years of experience, education and gut instinct, can provide the best possible advice in each situation presented to you. Stick to your principles and utilize the facts you have researched to present your position. It's only when you feel your principles will be compromised that should consider walking away from your current job and looking for a replacement. Remember at all times, it's your career to make or break. Any one company can enhance your career or ruin it—it's up to you.

... BUT WE DON'T PAY YOU LESS BECAUSE YOU'RE A WOMAN... WE PAY YOU LESS BECAUSE WE'RE MEN!
FRAN©

STEP FIVE

THE SACRED COW

Jesse always knew she would face obstacles in her career. Someone would be smarter, someone would have more experience, some men would always look at her as a woman and not a colleague, but she never thought she would face "the dreaded farm animal"! Yes, that funny looking sometimes spotted animal that moves slowly, makes funny mooing noises and represents cheese and chocolate malteds to some and filet mignon to others. The dreaded Sacred Cow! Now, if your religion requires this image to be worshipped, you are excused from this conversation, but all others listen up.

The Sacred Cow is alive and well and living in a company near you.

This problem is as troubling to women in their quest for advancement and success as it is to male executives working for the same goals. To add injury to insult, what if the sacred cow is a woman? What if she is sitting in a position of power and influence with the CEO in your company?

... Jesse walked down the hallway to the office of the CEO with important news about the planned public offering. She reached the CEO's office only to find, once again, his office door was closed. His assistant, Laura, was sitting at her desk.

"Can I see the boss?" Jesse asked.

"He is still meeting with Renee," Laura replied, smiling a telltale look that said here we go again.

"How long have they been in there?" Jesse was on a deadline and growing impatient.

"Two hours," Laura replied, "and he hasn't accepted any interruptions," she added.

Jesse knew that tone; Laura had tried several other important interruptions already with no success.

Renee was the company controller. An attractive 30- something, she was, from Jesse's point of view, a 5'5", slender woman with long blonde hair. She could be mistaken for a model; although most of the office gossip said the male staffers never considered Renee a very pretty girl, but that her figure carried her. (Need I say more!)

Renee was intelligent enough, but not the best option for controller. She was not a CPA, and Jesse, as staff to the CEO, held higher stature in the company. Jesse had no authority over Renee's position or her department.

Jesse often questioned the CEO about the strength of Renee's skills as a controller.

"She's doing a great job," he would say.

Jesse knew that a man with 30 years' experience in companies much larger that this should be a reliable judge of talent and skill.

"She just needs more coaching", he would continue. "I'm working on that with her all the time."

Jesse backed down, although she had pointed out poor-quality data and timing of information provided by Renee and her department. She could sense that a personal relationship stood in the way of the CEO's good judgment...

Years later, after interactions with several other sacred cows, Jesse wrote down her frustrations with the sacred cow. In her series of articles entitled "What Cow, Do You See One in the Room?", she revealed the secrets of these frustrations and how to work through and past them. These articles were used by many companies in an attempt to prevent the sacred cow from eating the grass in their pasture!

Excerpts from that series can help us learn how to face, battle, and then send the sacred cow to feed in someone else's pasture.

First let's define the sacred cow: this is a person within an organization who, for whatever reason (longevity, family relationship or personal attraction), is working for a company in a position of authority. This person does not possess the qualifications for the job and is entirely aware of their inadequacies. In order to cover for their lack of ability and related lack of self-confidence, the sacred cow responds with duplicitous behavior and undermines the efforts and successes of others. The goal of a sacred cow is to be the one the CEO turns to. He or she is enjoying the "free ride" from the accountability that most executives face every day.

In order to work the problem, there are five major steps to follow:

Step #1. IDENTIFY: Start by observing the actions and reactions of the one person you believe to be a sacred cow. Next, observe how other employees act around this person and react to this person. If you observe interactions that appear polite and supportive of the sacred cow, while reactions to this person's behavior are sarcastic and undermining when the sacred cow is not in the room, you have probably identified a true sacred cow. If you have a disagreement with the sacred cow while in a group and she defends herself by attacking you personally, you have found the true sacred cow in all her glory! During this disagreement, the rest of the group will either be silent or supportive of both parties in an effort to defuse the tension. The group knew something you didn't. They already knew about the sacred cow but forgot to tell you.

Step #2. ANALYZE: You have identified the sacred cow. It's time to step back, breathe deeply and forget all your anger and frustration. Use your analytical skills to assess the situation. Ask yourself, "What can the cow impact that directly affects my job?" or, "What can the cow influence that can hurt the company?" and lastly, "How can I counterbalance both so that I neutralize the effects of the cow." Work on this strategy and execute your plan without emotion. The employees will be grateful, even if the boss can't see the light.

Step #3. DON'T SPEAK: Yes, please don't speak. If the cow has been working for the company for more than six months, then the CEO surely has been "infected" with mad sacred-cow disease. The sacred cow has "his ear" and you will have a long, hard road ahead. If you shout from the rooftop, "She's a sacred cow, look out!", your words will fall on deaf ears, and you will be taken away in a straitjacket directly to the funny farm. Don't speak. Wait. Continue your business strategy, and keep your role and the company safe from the effects of the sacred cow's impact and influence. In time, the cow may move on to greener pastures.

Step #4. PRESENT THE FACTS: Always fall back on your two most important tools to success- the facts and the presentation of the facts. When you present these truths, the sacred cow will realize she is out of her league. She will resort to personal attacks and create mass hysteria to draw attention away from her incompetence. At some point, those in power will see the true face of the sacred cow.

Step #5. KNOW WHEN THE WALL IS TOO HIGH: If you have worked steps 1-4 and daily life has not changed, you will find yourself out of options. You will now be faced with presenting a frontal attack to the problem. Prepare yourself to walk away from the company in an effort to advance your career in a healthier environment. The CEO who ignores the truth about a sacred cow is missing some of the important qualities of a leader capable of carrying his company to sustained success. It really doesn't matter if the sacred cow is a man or a woman, or if the CEO is a man or a woman, leadership qualities are blind to gender. The male/female dynamic cannot be an excuse for poor leadership skills. A sacred cow cannot be tolerated under any circumstances. This is important enough to repeat: a sacred cow cannot be tolerated under any circumstances. If you present your argument in a factual presentation where your conclusions cannot be refuted, and the CEO refuses to acknowledge the problem or solve the problem, its time to work elsewhere!

Jesse walked, no ran, several times in her career, away from positions and into new ones. Sometimes the move was based on ethical grounds, sometimes on issues of respect and sometimes on her inability to move the CEO to action on a sacred cow.

When asked if she ever regretted her decisions to leave, she said, "No, my integrity and my sanity are always more important than the job." She continued:

"I knew my career and my success were entirely my responsibility and I could be successful no matter what role I played or where."

CEO at Last— Now What?

...Jesse sat at the head of the table. That was the traditional spot for the CEO in a board meeting. Today she claimed that all-important seat.

"Can they see the fear on my face?" she wondered. "Can they hear my heart pounding? I don't know if this is excitement or horror. How did I finally get this job? Whose idea was this anyway?"

Jesse was deep in thought when the other board members filed slowly into the room. One by one Jesse looked at them, knew each one by name and knew their long history with the company. She smiled a soft smile of appreciation. After all, it wasn't more than a month ago that the former CEO resigned and the board voted her into the role. Having been the CFO and Senior Vice President for more than three years, she deserved the job and no one doubted it. She was sure she understood her new role and was quite passionate about the challenges ahead. It was her turn at the head of the table. She only wished she could read the minds of every member of the board and every member of her executive team.

Preparation, Planning and Pondering

Jesse prepared for the board meeting for the two weeks prior to the event. She pored over every number, analyzed every strength, every trend; she was always the numbers person.

"Jesse could put together those numbers and see into the operation with clarity better than any CFO I ever knew," said Charles, the former CEO.

Charles had been CEO for more than twelve years. He had the smarts to utilize the talents of those around him. Charles was one who constantly learned from all the sources he could find to help guide him to success.

Jesse also learned from Charles and followed his lead, studying the greats in management and leadership training. She wanted to bring all the right values, principles and characteristics to the job of CEO. Through the years, with many lessons learned and many lessons that went unlearned, Jesse refused to be one of those women who achieved a position of power and let it go to her head! Too many women along the way had achieved the position at the top, just to have it, and them, destroyed by greed, jealousy, obsession with success for success's sake, or a sense of revenge against the men who were in the way.

Wow, this is starting to sound like a trashy, made for TV movie! Sorry, I digress. Back to Jesse...

As part of Jesse's daily preparation for her role as CEO she did a few things:

First, she would get up in the morning and read her passion statement. She called it that because it was a blend of mission, vision, dream, longing and excitement statements. This paragraph or two covered not only her work role, but her family, social, spiritual and health roles. This was her life statement. When she read this page she felt her heart and soul stir within her. It was passion in every sense of the word.

Second, Jesse would close her eyes and see the faces of those she wanted to thank. She saw her husband, her children, her parents and her mentors. She felt the presence of her God. She needed to do this because, without gratitude to those who were such important parts of her life, success would be meaningless.

Third, she would take a half-hour to write down any new ideas or strategic paths she had thought of during the night. Sometimes if you go to bed with a problem, your subconscious mind will solve it while you are sleeping. (You know, that busy part of your brain that never sleeps!) Those answers, thoughts, approaches and lessons need to be written down before your work brain takes over for the day.

Then Jesse was ready for the day. On the first inside page of Jesse's journal was a list of important words. Every time she opened the journal to write, she saw them. These were her reminders, words that represented the values, principles and characteristics she wanted with her at all times. Let's take a look at Jesse's journal:

Tools of a CEO

Build Into Your Character

- ✓ Humility
- ✓ Open-Mindedness
- ✓ Accessibility
- ✓ Tempered Judgment
- ✓ Even-Handedness
- ✓ Sense of Reality
- ✓ Team Building: No isolation —No Man or Woman is an Island
- ✓ Determined and Full of Myself?

Great CEOs nurture leaders then listen to them.

Dictators create and demand an abundance of followers who will never lead.

Jesse often reflected on this list and, now, waiting for that first board meeting, she was taken back to each of those words. From this day forward, each word would be vital to her successful role as a CEO. Her judges were not just inside that board room, they were every employee in the company, and every financial partner the company had, the "street" in its judgmental ways and, lastly, the press. A woman CEO in the world of corporate America was a novelty, and the press was quick to analyze that CEO's every move, good or bad. Because of the many guides Jesse had over her long career, her ability to manage the new role was assured. The big question would be, did Jesse have the internal fortitude to do what she knew she could?

HUMILITY—(noun): modest or respectfulness; the quality of being modest or respectful.

Humility in business, as in life, holds two meanings: 1. Remember where you came from when you were not in charge, and were learning from those around you and, 2. Never treat others with a lack of respect. If you are the leader, the lives of those around you are important too. You must respect the front desk operator as much as you respect the chairman of the board.

OPEN-MINDEDNESS—(noun); free from prejudice and receptive to new ideas.

The way you became successful is by presenting the facts of your case to an open-minded person. The only reason you have been successful is because you were open to learning from others in positions of leadership. Don't stop now. You will always need to learn from those around you. From peers, mentors, coaches and, yes, the team that works for you today. You chose them for their abilities; don't walk away from their advice when it counts the most. The brutal honesty of those who care can provide the right tools to help you make good choices every day.

ACCESSIBILITY—(noun): approachable; not aloof and not difficult to talk or meet with.

When you are the boss, your assistant must control where you spend your time and with whom. You need to be accessible to those people who help you every day. I am not talking about constant interruptions. I am talking about an actual state of mind. If the culture in your company says the boss is hard to get in to see, then the mental picture is: the boss is cut off from my ideas and an honest and open interaction about any issue. You can actually discourage communication on important issues if you are not available to your team.

TEMPERED JUDGMENT—Tempered (adjective): well-proportioned, with elements combined in balance and suitable proportion. Judgment (noun): good sense; the ability to form sound opinions and make sensible decisions or reliable guesses.

When you rely on the ability to form good, sound opinions with elements combined in balance, you get a person who can weigh all options before making a decision. When a CEO takes information from one recommended source and ignores information from all others, she is not using tempered judgment. The perception of favoritism or "approach over substance" becomes the culture of the executive floor and can permeate throughout the organization if not kept in check. If the vendor with the right connections says the words the CEO wants to hear or provides that magic bullet to success, a CEO, without tempered judgment, will fall for it every time. Take time to breathe. Weigh all options, well-presented or not. Someone is trying to tell you something, and you have to be open to hear it.

EVENHANDEDNESS—(adjective): fair, unbiased; treating everyone fairly without favoritism or discrimination.

An evenhanded management style is a necessary tool in your arsenal, especially for a woman. Showing favoritism to the words and opinions of one woman or man who works for you can cloud your judgment. If one person "has your ear" and can unfairly influence a decision, your ability to lead the company is impaired. Stay away from reliance solely on the sacred cow or your right-hand man, both of whom might have significantly more access to you than their peers. Use good judgment and rely on the facts when making decisions. Those facts carried you *to* the position and they will carry you *in* the position.

SENSE OF REALITY—reality (noun): keep well-grounded; actual being or existence, as opposed to an imaginary, idealized, or false nature.

The kids today say "keep it real." I think they are onto something. In business, we can look at reality all around us, or we can believe that people can be more or do more or act differently than they do today. The financial world gives us tools to help us measure reality. Those tools include historical trends. They help us see the past as we attempt to predict the future. A company with historical trends that shows they accomplish "X" cannot be expected to accomplish "Y" in the next year.

Reality. A brick wall will always be a brick wall. You can paint it, plant flowers in front of it, put ceramic pots on top of it, and it will still be a brick wall. If you really want a wooden fence, you must be prepared to break down the brick wall with a very large sledgehammer in replace it with a wooden fence.

Your business is that brick wall. The way the team operates, performs functions and expounds company philosophy is a brick wall. If you want something different from that brick wall, you are not guided by a sense of reality. Small adjustments can happen without breaking the wall, but major shifts in perspective and culture will need a very large sledgehammer to accomplish change.

TEAM BUILDING—team (noun): a number of people organized to function cooperatively as a group toward a common goal. Build (verb): to make something by joining parts.

You can take a group of like-minded people who all desire to work toward a common goal and give them a sense of organization by joining them in some form that accentuates each of their abilities to contribute to the common good. A good leader nurtures the talents of the individual and guides these talents toward the single purpose set forth in the common goal. So, in English this time: Take the best of the best, nurture their personal talents and bring them together for a common goal! Let them loose to bring new, fresh and objective ideas for success, then listen to them.

DETERMINED and **FULL OF MYSELF**—Determined, (adjective): with fixed purpose; feeling or showing firmness.

As a last important reflection, Jesse runs a self-check and asks herself, "Am I determined or full of myself?" This question is her reality check.

"I know that a strong- willed, determined, goal-oriented driver is what it takes to succeed," she might say, "but have I gone too far? Let me always consider; do I think more of myself than I should? I know my face is the one the world sees every day, but do I get all the credit or do I always remember those who helped and still do?"

When you read the greatest success stories throughout history you will notice that self-glorification is missing from each personality we revere. When power goes to your head, you lose all you have created. There are several good books that discuss leadership, power and the full-of-myself mentality. I recommend the following to any and all aspiring leaders, male and female. Once you fall into the traps of the full-of-myself mentality, you become susceptible to all the major pitfalls of stardom. What are they? Well, that's a good subject for another book!

As Jesse finishes her morning notes, she turns back to the first page in her journal and reads aloud:

"Great CEOs nurture leaders then listen to them; dictators create and demand an abundance of followers who will never lead"

Now she is ready to meet the board. The rest is history.

Role Playing to Help Move Your Career Forward

Job; Career; Life; Reach for it!

Many years ago Jesse sat in her college classes wondering:

"Where will I be working in the next ten years?"

Usually, while a nervous student sits patiently waiting to start the CPA exam, the last thing she is thinking about is, "Will I become a CFO or a partner in a national CPA Firm?" But, while Jesse sat in her office almost 18 years after that important test, she pondered many things. "Where is my career going next?" It was at that point in time she realized her job was not her career, and her career was not her life. So much of her time was spent making the dreams of those around her a reality that she didn't think much about her own dreams. Her approach to the question "What are your goals in life?" was to answer, "My goals are to make the goals of others a reality."

After graduate school, Jesse did what most graduate accounting school students do, she went to work for the, then, "Big Eight". She could still hear the words of her graduate school professor, "You always start with Big Eight. From there you can go anywhere, but from anywhere else, you can't go to the Big Eight." Jesse was sought after. She interviewed with many of those firms and got offers from three of them. She chose one. How did she decide? She made her decision based on the fact that this one firm actually helped her with her graduate thesis. The interviewer had the firm's reproduction department make copies of her thesis while Jesse finished her interview. This made Jesse feel special, and by the way, helped her meet her deadlines!

The firm, one of the biggest, was a great starting place for anyone's career. Jesse took that job very seriously, and every assignment became the most important thing in her life. When it came time to move on, she had to choose between a different firm or a different city.

Jesse joined a smaller firm with a large office in the new city. Again, the firm became her whole life. Each assignment and the people she worked with were her lifeblood. Throughout this time, Jesse gained knowledge and experience in her career.

Auditing, of course, can take you just so far, especially if you do not aspire to become a partner in the firm. Jesse realized that she wanted to utilize her talents within one company, to help nurture the growth and development of one company, making her way from management to executive. Again, each job Jesse took became the most important thing in her life.

Along the way, Jesse married and had a family. Her husband and children had to fit into her nice, neat segregation of time and energy because, after all, the job, the company, was most important. She had to work on that public offering, go on that road show, and involve herself in every aspect of the operation. Every decision process was personal. The success of the company was her ultimate goal.

Slowly, Jesse began to lose touch with her professional network and the rest of the business community. As each company came and went, due to mergers, sales and dissolutions, Jesse tried to find the path to the one company that could be her lifeblood, that she could make a success.

Each time, the company or the job disappointed her in one way or the other. Whether it was the entrepreneur who didn't have enough vision, the parent company that wanted the subsidiary to do things their way or the lack of financial wherewithal to carry the company to the next level, Jesse was continually disappointed.

So, 18 years into her career she reached an impasse. She had spent the past six years devoting herself to a company that promised to be *her* company. As CFO, she had once again made it her life blood, excluding all else.

Again, the company disappointed. Changes in ownership and direction created the obvious—the decision to move on. Jesse decided for once to sit back and look at her future. Where was she going next? Was every job going to be the same? The answer was NO.

It was time to look at her career and decide how she was going to work on the growth and development of her future career, not her next job.

Jesse focused on her expertise in Financial Management, whether as a CPA, CFO, business consultant, teacher, writer, speaker, it didn't matter. Jesse spent the next few years as a work in progress. For the first time, she was working on her dreams and visions, not the visions of her latest boss.

The realization that family is important comes to individuals at different points in their lives. Some women always know that they want to be a stay-at-home mom. Some feel a career is very important. Balance in these two areas is also compounded by the need to be a full-time partner with your spouse. Men in society have struggled with the job overwhelming home life for many years. Recently, men have come to realize that they can be part of the family too, helping with doctor appointments for the kids and coaching baseball, as well as having a full-time job.

Women have always struggled with the battle between the office and the home. They are usually the parent who makes dinner, yet fulfills their work obligation. Jesse faced many nine to ten-hour workdays that required a great deal of efficiency and effectiveness, because she didn't have the luxury of working overtime. Also, her office had to be portable, so she could work at home after her boys went to bed!

Fast-forward to that author and lecturer standing in front of the university hall. Jesse smiled with pride. She finally felt like a success. Her career had morphed past a mere job and became simply a piece of her life-her successful life, filled with rewarding relationships and an ability to help other women succeed in their careers, in their lives.

Part II: The Arrival

The Test: Take the Glass Ceiling Quiz and Analyze Your Answers

Take the Quiz and let's see where you stand on the steps of the Ladder to Success!

Here are some important tips to remember as you prepare to take this quiz:

- Don't take yourself too seriously, have fun with the quiz and yourself!
- Take a good, honest look at each question and decide what you would do if you were in that situation. The important words here are GOOD and HONEST! No one is going to judge you except you and, if you are honest, you can only improve.

- Don't ask your friends' opinions on how you should answer; this is not their quiz, it's yours. How your friends see you is not nearly as important as how you see yourself.

- Once you finish the quiz, add up your points and read the assessment of your overall score. Then go to the analysis of each question and each answer to see why one answer is better than another. Some questions will have two good answers; but, to break the glass ceiling, the best answer will sometimes be more difficult to implement. Do it anyway. If you are going to go for it, then give it your all; Passion, Drive and Perseverance are the key words in getting the job done!

I know, enough already, just a few more important points. Take these thoughts with you after you finish the book and put it away on your shelf.

- **LEARN** from your mistakes—That means don't just make the mistake and forget it; learn from it, make the correction of the mistake a part of your future plans. Write down the lesson in your journal, if you must, but write it down. Did I tell you to keep a journal? You should!

- **PASSION**—Everything you do, do it with passion. If you don't have passion for what you are doing then you are doing the wrong thing!

- **LOGIC AND FACT**—Approach each and every argument in favor of your position with logic and fact. Take out the emotion. If you know why others act the way they do then you know their position and presentation is not a personal attack. Logic and fact will keep your emotions in check and deflect any perception of personal attack

- **EMBARRASSMENT**—Don't embarrass your staff, peers or the boss, ever! Discipline in private, admonish in private, praise in public.

- **FRUSTRATION**—Get rid of it. It doesn't help, ever!

- **SELF-CONFIDENCE**—If you believe in yourself and your talent then self-confidence will shine through. If you have self-confident then no-one else's tactics can throw you off your game

Time for the Quiz....

Multiple-Choice Questions:

1) EXPERIENCE: How many years' experience do you have in your current field or profession?

a. Five or less

b. Five to ten

c. Over ten

d. None—still a student

2) POSITION: What level are you today?

a. Employee

b. Manager

c. Executive

d. Student

3) SO MANY JOBS, SO LITTLE TIME: How many jobs have you had in the last six (6) years?

a. Two

b. Three

c. More than three

d. One

Ok, those were the EASY questions!

4) IS YOUR BOSS A DICTATOR? You are faced with the following: The boss says: "Do your job because I say so, don't question my decision!" Although you don't agree with his decision, you respond:

a. Yes sir! I always agree with the boss.

b. Understood, but please evaluate these points and reconsider your decision.

c. Hell with you! I don't agree.

d. Sure. The boss knows best, right? So it's best if I don't question his decisions even if I don't agree.

5) MONEY OR AUTHORITY? You have a chance to interview for a new position in your current company. The position offers a 10% increase in pay and a new title, same boss, but no real change in authority, OR you can take a new job offer that has a 5% increase in pay, new title and lots of input on the development of a new program. What should you do?

a. Take the 10% raise. Who cares if you get any real say? Its all about the money, isn't it?

b. Take the promotion. You can always hope to make a difference once you have the job. Really, it's not about the money.

c. It's time to move on and advance. Take the new job and start moving your career forward.

d. Talk to your boss about the promotion and explain the goal of real change, the need to gain real authority with the promotion.

6) CONTROL ISSUES: Who pushes your buttons? (Who is in control?)

a. I AM! I always evaluate how I can make my points, the same way a man would, so the CEO can accept my advice without feeling like he is "listening to mommy!"

b. That MALE PEER! He's always getting away with making mistakes. I tried to tell the boss. I yelled, stomped my feet and told him that guy's ideas would just cost more money. Man, I get so mad!

c. MY BOSS! He never listens, so I just stopped talking, stopped participating. I'm hurt because he won't take me seriously.

7) **DRESS FOR SUCCESS:** What to wear? Here is your profile: 34 years old, 5'5" tall, 125 lbs, MBA graduate in Marketing and Economics, currently the Assistant Director of Business Development for a mid-size private company. *Dress for Success* says I should wear?

a. The Latest Fashion—short-sassy skirt, hug-the-hips, fitted T-shirt and short jacket. Hey if it works for "The Apprentice" then it should work for me!

b. Fashion Plus Professional—I shop at the business clothes stores for skirts and pantsuits, fitted, but not glued to my body, worn with a nice button-down shirt that is buttoned to show no cleavage.

c. Comfort - oversize skirt, big, bulky sweater. I like natural fabrics. I don't like the fashion look because I am against corporate judgments.

d. Not Sure —I wear what is in my closet because people should appreciate my mind, not my clothes.

8) THE BIG PRESENTATION: You have the opportunity to speak before a large group of your peers and senior members of your industry. The topic is one you know very well and are fluent in presenting within your own company. You like the thought of being in front of the rooms so what are the most important things to remember before you make the presentation?

a. Know your material better than ever but have notes, even if you think you can wing it.

b. Test your speaking and presenting equipment before the speech. The worst presentations occur when the microphone doesn't work and your power point can't be seen because the projector is broken.

c. Speak clearly and loudly enough to be heard. Presentations from those who speak softly bore the audience

d. All of the above. A good presenter is always prepared.

9) THE BUSINESS LUNCH: You are scheduled to meet with the boss in the office at 11a.m. for your regularly scheduled one-to-one monthly meeting. He is running late that day and tells his assistant to have you meet him at a local restaurant at 11:45 for your meeting. He sees this as a way to meet and have food at the same time. What do you do?

a. Make an excuse and reschedule the meeting. You never have lunch alone with the boss. This is your rule.

b. Go to the lunch. Spend some time on business but relax and spend some time talking about your relationship with your spouse. After all, the boss is older and smarter than you and he may have some good marital advice

c. Go to lunch and bring your agenda and business notes. Stick to business and sit across the table from him as you in the office. Participate in a productive meeting. Recommend that you set future meeting times earlier in the day to prevent confusion in scheduling.

d. Explain to the boss's assistant that you don't lunch with the boss alone. It's not appropriate and could she reschedule.

10) HOW TO SOCIALIZE: You have three departments working for you, a mixture of male and female managers and staff. You are the COO. The group is having an afterwork get-together at a local restaurant and bar to celebrate a manager's birthday. What do you do?

a. Stop in for one drink and some appetizers; be nice, polite but not too friendly. Drive to the event in your own vehicle so you can control the interaction.

b. Go to the event with another executive who is male, say hello, have one drink and let your male counterpart drive you home.

c. Stay the whole time, drink and enjoy. After all, it's your departments that are celebrating, and you consider this team building. If you get a little tipsy, well, it's to be expected. Have private conversations with other managers about how upset you are with the CEO this week!

d. Stay, party, be friendly, and share personal information with your team. It helps them feel close to you. Don't lose control but be part of the group.

11) DO YOU HAVE A SACRED COW? The business is facing tough times: The company is headed into a down market, and those responsible for sales are not doing their job. The CEO and sales director have worked together for years and are very close. How do you help the company?

a. Continue providing information, stats and trends, over and over. Keep recommending ways to increase sales.

b. Privately tell the CEO that you are concerned by the numbers and trends for sales, and the job performance of the sale director. Recommend new paths without really addressing the sales director's ability to do the job.

c. Embarrass the sales director in meetings every chance you get. Your job is to hold people accountable, no matter how bad it looks. You see this as team pressure for results.

d. Give several face-saving alternatives to the CEO in private. Explain that no matter the relationship, change is necessary.

12) ADVANCEMENT: You already work for a female CFO and she isn't going anywhere soon. You have presented several good changes and programs to help with cost control and revenue opportunities in your company, but you feel no progress in your career, what do you do?

a. Look for possible lateral moves out of Finance into Treasury, Marketing, Operations or Internal Audit; all in an effort to skip over the CFO but stay with the company.

b. Look at your skill level and assess how much more you can learn in the current position before you make a decision to move on.

c. Go all out and find a new opportunity today. Don't waste time in a job with no chance at the CFO role anytime soon.

d. Stay for today, constantly create and maintain contacts, learn how to network inside your company and outside in your profession. When the right move shows itself, you will be ready.

e. All of the above.

13) OPPORTUNITY FOR STARDOM: You are presented with the opportunity to hold a position on the governing board of your business or industry trade organization. You would love to take this role but some peer in your own company, who has very loose lips, is also part of this group. Should you take the position?

a. Yes, take the position.

b. No, wait for an opportunity with a different organization.

14) BATTLE THE SACRED COW: The company has one person who has passion and drive, but no ability to close the deal. Everyone loves this person but secretly everyone wonders when the CEO is going to make this person as accountable as the rest of the team. What should you do?

a. Ignore the sacred cow. Work around them and focus on your job. Let them be someone else's problem.

b. Question the CEO about the sacred cow, over and over, until the CEO gets the message. He will know you are doing the right thing for the company.

c. Facts and the Presentation of the Facts: Give the boss all the proper documentation regarding results, missed deadlines and mismanaged staff without personal commentary. You know he's smart and will make the right decision.

d. Take out your resume and polish it. If the boss hasn't figured out the sacred cow stuff by now, he never will. It's time for you to advance your career somewhere else.

15) IT'S TIME TO BE CEO: After 15 years in your profession and roles as COO, VP Marketing, VP Product Development and VP Regional Business Development, you feel you are ready to take over the role of CEO in this company or another. What course of action will play out to be most favorably to get you that next promotion up the ladder?

a. Continue to work hard and someone will realize you deserve the role of CEO.

b. Send a personal letter and a copy of your resume to each member of the Board of Directors. If they are looking to replace the CEO, they will know that you are available and ready for the job.

c. Find a good headhunter who can look for positions on your behalf in a blind solicitation. They can find a fit for you without upsetting your current position. They may even find you are the one to replace your current boss!

Scoring Point Totals:

Answer / Points	Answer / Points	Answer / Points
1) a 3	6) a 10	11) a 3
b 10	b 2	b 5
c 5	c 3	c 0
d 2		d 10
	7) a 0	
2) a 3	b 10	12) a 5
b 5	c 2	b 5
c 10	d 5	c 3
d 2		d 5
	8) a 5	e 10
3) a 10	b 5	
b 3	c 5	13) a 0
c 2	d 10	b 10
d 5		
	9) a 3	14) a 5
4) a 3	b 0	b 0
b 10	c 10	c 10
c 2	d 5	d 10
d 5		
	10) a 10	15) a 3
5) a 2	b 5	b 0
b 3	c 0	c 10
c 10	d 0	
d 5		

Scoring:

20 to 50 points: It appears that you need a significant amount of guidance if you want a career in corporate America. This may not be your passion and you might consider taking your creative side in another direction.

51 to 100 points: There is room to improve, so continue to work on your interpersonal skills and self-confidence.

101 to 150 points: Your judgment and self-confidence are in the right places and you are ready to go all the way. Glass is breaking all around you!

Analyze the Answers:

Question #1 Experience

In order to progress in your career you have to understand where you stand today. Time and effort play important roles in your progress. Stardom before your time usually spells doom.

a. In five or fewer years you have acquired the basics of your profession and may have a good foundation for success. You may have already faced challenges such as the man/woman dynamic, the sacred cow and the lack of listening skills we find in men who need to listen to smart women.

A compounding problem is your youth. Youth will be a drawback for any woman wanting to move quickly. If you are a fast tracker then use your business tools and your "cool" to help move you along the track as fast as possible.

b. Having between five and ten years experience puts you in the best position to move quickly along the path of your career. Apply the business tools you possess to keep from wasting time. It would be wise to look at your current position and make the necessary moves during the time that counts the most.

c. If you have more than ten years' experience, the big question is "Where are you now?" If you are over ten years and not that far along, the best approach is back to the basics. Consider all the positions you have held in the past ten years and evaluate the good, the bad and the ugly of those jobs. This would be the time to learn from the lessons on the table, find a better direction and move forward. Break a little glass and head for the top of the ladder.

d. Students are in a great position to make things happen. By choosing your goals today, you will already be on a path that took your predecessors years to understand. Use every advantage, from new technology to good common sense to help you get started. Read about and observe women who have made it in your profession. Learn from them, skip over their mistakes and hit the ground running!

Question #2 Position

a. As an employee you are ready to soak up knowledge from all around you, including other employees, managers and executives. These are your learning years. At this point in your career, going the extra mile when "it's not my job", can advance you faster than most on the ladder to success.

b. Manager is the most unappreciated and unnoticed position in business. Use this time to figure out your game plan and execute.

c. Executive. If you are sitting at the big table and reading this book, good for you! The only way to achieve real success and break through the glass ceiling is to live the role of a real executive and not just own the title. The CEO of today is just a role model, good or bad, for your role tomorrow. Your goal is to be better than any man in a man's world, no male bashing intended. The fact is that if you, as a woman, want the title CEO, you have to do it better, faster, smarter, and with more insight and excellent mastery of the tools, than your male counterpart. Get started now because mastery of the tools is very hard work!

d. Student. Read everything twice. You have the opportunity to move twice as fast as your predecessors.

Question #3 So Many Jobs, So Little Time!

a. Two jobs in six years is a good record and will establish that you are a stable individual. In most cases, more than four years inside one company, in one job, is stagnating. As CEO, you could run a company for seven to ten years in order to mature your long-term strategy. Short of CEO, most executives in support positions will need a new major role within the same organization, or in a new company, within the first five years as executive.

b. Holding three jobs in six years says you are flighty and unstable. Try not to move around so much unless outside forces such as the economy cause companies to close.

c. More than three: Are you sure you're working in your chosen profession? You might want to consider another field or go back to school. You're not a happy person if you're jumping jobs every six months.

d. One position in six years: This is preferable in the early years, but six years is a long time without a promotion. Take a good look at your passion statement and ask yourself why you aren't farther along on your journey. Once you know the answer, be honest and set a plan of attack.

Question #4 Is your Boss a Dictator?

a. A yes-woman is just as bad as a yes-man! If you are enamored with the boss's strengths, then learn them and use them to help build your own strengths. You must have an opinion or you are just window dressing.

b. This is a good answer! Have your facts ready so you can provide alternatives and considerations. You might not change his mind, but you will be ready for the outcome. Although, if you realize this is his working style, you may consider looking for another job.

c. Pack your bags, the frontal attack never works!

d. Lack of self-confidence in your ability will turn your head around in self-doubt. Do your homework and stand your ground in a professional manner. Your career needs by an open-minded boss. Your next move is to start the search for a new position but, first, lose the scared mouse approach.

Question #5 Money or Authority

a. Today, maybe it's about money. Tomorrow, when you wake up and go to work in the same place you were before, how much enthusiasm can you really have for the job?

b. Fooling yourself never works. Be realistic; if you are taking the job for money, at least acknowledge it. If you cannot be honest with yourself, you will spend years being dishonest with others.

c. This is part of the big picture. Your passion statement will drive you to leave and pursue real growth!

d. You may be able to gain ground internally. If you do stay, you will spend an inordinate amount of time working on gaining authority. This will overwhelm your actual work performance. Hoping for change is another form of denying the truth. Don't confuse this with being hopeful in life. Life is full of hope. This position is not. It's lacking a sense of reality.

Question #6 Control Issues

a. Yes! You are in control. For better or for worse, you are 100% responsible to make it happen or let it fail. All of us face challenges every day, but when you realize you control the impact of each and every challenge in your life, you win!

b. Why is there always one guy or girl who pushes your buttons? The answer is "that's life." Now, if you give control of your life over to that very same person, you might as well give up your dreams today and resign yourself to a life of ordinary times.

c. Withdraw and he wins. The boss is the boss, that's his job. You are the boss of your own life. This may not be where your voice will be heard, but that doesn't mean stop speaking! Speak where your voice will be heard.

Question #7 Dress for Success

a. Hollywood and the fashion district of New York City are not the best measurements to determine the dress-for-success approach. Too tight is just that, too tight, even if you are only a size two! Short skirts only beg a man to look at a woman's figure instead of the woman.

b. Yes! You can look great and businesslike if you wear what fits, with style. No excess cleavage, please; remember this when you lean forward over a desk and a man can see what your blouse isn't covering! The male mind is reminded of sex every day by TV and movies. Your job is to focus on facts and presentation and keep his mind on his job!

c. Baggy is just not smart. Forget corporate judgment, you still need to present the corporate image. You would never see the male CEO of a major corporation at a board of directors meeting in corduroy pants and a baggy sweater.

d. Don't use the mind-over-looks argument because you think it's too expensive to look good. In cities all across the country you can find outlet malls and stores where fashion meets bargain pricing. I didn't say expensive, I just said fashionable.

Question #8 The Most Important Presentation

a. Knowing the material to present in front of coworkers is not the same as presenting to strangers, so be prepared.

b. Your presentation is well-received whey you look as prepared as you feel.

c. No one likes to strain to hear you or to decipher your words because you are mumbling or rambling. Stay on point. The participant's time is as valuable as your time, so make it count. Would you want to listen to stories about grandpa's fishing trip, even if it has a cool message?

d. Yes. Do all these things and your presentation skills will aid you in building rapport, contacts, and that all-important self-confidence so you can move forward in your career.

Question #9 The Business Lunch

a. This may work as an emergency fix, but at some point in time you may have to face the challenge.

b. Lunch is not a counseling session. The more personal baggage you give your boss, the less he sees you as a qualified executive. He may want to care for you, but he won't promote you.

c. Yes! Good judgment will prevail. Professional actions will save the day.

d. Your boss may see this as an insult, and out of the inner circle you go.

Question #10 Socialize

a. Yes. Don't act like a snob but remember: you are the boss, not a buddy. Good rapport with your team can be rewarding. As long as you respect yourself, the team will respect you. Always utilize your own vehicle so you can control where you go, when and with whom.

b. No matter how innocent your working relationship is with your male executive teammates, you will still leave your staff with the impression of impropriety if you leave the event with a male executive.

c. If you picked c, you will wake up with a hangover and the need to look for another job! Never be the life of the party. Loose lips sink careers.

d. If your boss is not your counselor, then your employees are also not counselors. The more the staff knows about your personal life, the less respect they have for you as an executive.

Question #11 Do You Have a Sacred Cow?

a. Frustration will be ever present in your life if you continue to hope that this time your information will cause the CEO to make a change.

b. Tiptoe around if you must, but you are not doing your job if you are not honest with the CEO.

c. Never embarrass, ever! This is so hard. All you do is create a hostile work environment and never solve the problem. You look like the problem now instead of the ever-present cow holding that title/taking the blame!

d. Yes. Stretch your skills to a new level by providing real solutions. Be honest with the CEO in recommending change, but show how it can be done gracefully.

Question #12 Advancement

a. A lateral move can be a good option. Learning more about your company from inside another department may not get you the CFO or CEO role, but you and your resume will benefit from the experience.

b. This is also a good move. To really understand where you are in the learning curve before you make a move will help you make the right move.

c. No time is better than the present to test the waters. Be discreet since most corporate executives know someone who knows someone close to your company.

d. Patience and persistence will keep you from jumping ship right into a leaky boat! Networking your contacts brings long-term benefits.

e. This choice is the best choice because each of the approaches listed will work out, depending on the current stage of your career.

Question #13 Stardom

a. This would be a bad choice. No matter how professional you try to remain in any and all interactions, the other person will find a way to bring gossip into the picture and back to the company. Avoid this interaction at all costs.

b. Yes, stay away. There are many trade or professional organizations to choose from in order to advance your career and avoid any unpleasant experiences.

Question #14 Battle the Sacred Cow (again?)

a. The silent treatment never works. If you ignore the problems, they will just keep growing.

b. Wow, are you annoying! The boss doesn't want to hear it, so catch on and don't repeat yourself.

c. Yes, the facts and presentation of the facts give you the best opportunity for success.

d. This is also a true statement, but you must face the hard truth. Your career will be better served if you make a change.

Question #15 Are You CEO Material?

a. This is wishful thinking. The only person who is looking out for you is you.

b. This is too forward. The board of directors respects loyalty and they will see your approach as disloyal to your boss.

c. This is a very good answer. You are marketable, so let the experts market you when you are ready.

Now that you have worked through all of these issues and have a fair understanding of your current position on the ladder, how much glass have you broken? If you say not nearly enough then you have work to do. If you are an executive with high aspirations to be CEO, I hope this quick look at some commonsense concepts will be helpful to you.

It's been fun, and I am always looking for feedback. E-mail me your comments and questions at ddutton@writebookstoday.com. I look forward to watching you break through the glass ceiling into the top seats in corporate America today!

Knowledge: The Eight Most Important Business Fallacies —What Are They and Why Are They in Your Career Path?

Business Fallacy #1: The Knee-Jerk Reaction

Have you ever seen a boss just after he discovered some specific problem with a business issue or event? Bosses experience this strong desire to solve the problem instantly, without looking at the big picture. This phenomenon is called the Knee-Jerk Reaction.

Why does this happen? It happens because bosses are insecure in their ability to manage the overall business. If they were confident, they would have been prepared for downturns in business trends, personnel issues, breakdowns in mechanical devises, and on and on and on. The day-to-day pressures of a business can fry the brains of even the best bosses, but those that remain cool, level headed and "on plan" will be the ones who succeed long-term.

You, as the recipient of the Knee-Jerk Reaction, have to be ready for anything. You can make this reaction fit into the plan for the business by pointing out that an impromptu layoff or slashing the maintenance budget or selling off inventory in a fire sale are the wrong answers to the immediate problem.

If you are a good advisor, this is your time to shine. A projection of the outcome of this reaction vs. staying on course, or changing the long-term strategy of the company will help to bring sanity to moments of insanity. No boss facing the facts will continue on a course of action that is detrimental to the overall business health of the company in question. You can actually steer the company in the right direction—right out of a Knee-Jerk Reaction.

Business Fallacy #2: Loyalty Above All

Have you ever run across the employee who has worked for the company for so many years they are part of the furniture? That one person who really doesn't have a job description, just kind of does what the boss wants done? Or the person who is in charge of a department just because they have held the position for five years while the company grew from 25 people to 300. Now they appear very much in over their head. Sometimes this person has several important business skills and an understanding of their industry but very little ability to see a project to a profitable long term conclusion.

This person can be called a sacred cow, or just someone working outside or beyond his or her potential. This person is there because they are LOYAL to the company and or the owner.

Loyalty is a very important business concept. BUT—it's not the answer to a successful business. A good boss can distinguish when loyalty alone starts to cause damage to the company. When a company outgrows its employees and keeps them in place because of their loyalty, the company loses perspective on its goals for success.

As a person having the ear of the boss, you need to objectively and factually point to the qualities lacking in the loyal employee, and either find a place where they can contribute or force the realization that this person has outstayed their welcome. If a boss is faced with the facts, once again they will make the right decision.

Business Fallacy #3: Working Beyond Someone's Potential

An individual has the capacity to do many things; some can reach beyond their anticipated potential and show themselves to be more than what was expected of them. Some reach a certain ceiling and can do no more. It is important that leadership realizes this fact and works within the capacity of those employees who have reached their limit.

This is not fun, the boss usually wants just that little bit more from the people they have. Sometimes this causes problems with their employees. The average employee is just that, an employee. They punch a clock in most cases; they don't own the company, so when they go home at night the last thing they are worrying about is the success or failure of the company they work for. Their biggest concern is what football game is on this weekend, or their place on the bowling league.

Trying to work someone beyond his or her potential is a sure plan for failure. It's also a sure plan for ulcers and stress-related illnesses for the employee. Being an executive advisor, you must guide management in realizing the potential of the employee pool, putting each employee in the proper position and working them to their utmost potential, giving them a sense of purpose, not frustration. This will not only provide you with happy employees, but also give you the most bang for the buck!

Business Fallacy #4: The Inability to Confront Inept Performance

Do you find that the boss doesn't confront those employees whose performances you see as inept? Have you asked yourself WHY doesn't he deal with these people? Good question. This is a tough answer to find. The answer might lie in the personality of the boss. The answer might lie in human nature. Human nature says be nice to people so they will like you. I once worked for a company president who told me that the more people didn't like me, the more he knew I was doing my job.

Human nature says the boss should be liked, which equals respect in their minds. Even if it means never confronting those who are inept.

You can spend many hours in total frustration over this issue, or you can find a way to direct the circumstances so that the inept employee is exposed for just that. In that case, the boss is never the bad guy. You are. That's okay—you're tough enough to take it because your overall result is a successful company that provides jobs for employees and profits for owners. And those inept employees? Usually they move on to provide their inept services to some other unsuspecting employer.

Business Fallacy #5: Mr. Nice Guy

Throughout these business fallacies, it appears that I am picking on the boss. This is true. The biggest problem with business today is who is managing it. In many cases you have the boss who grew up with the business and has no training in management. Sometimes you have a CEO who is just a little full of himself. So what does this create? Usually a Mr. Nice Guy.

This image as a manager is definitely a business fallacy. Mr. Nice Guy plays to certain select audiences, mostly those he or she is trying to impress. Those people closest to Mr. Nice Guy, those people Mr. Nice Guy relies on, rarely see the Mr. Nice Guy image. They see the cut-to-the-chase, make it happen or else image.

So what do we think of Mr. Nice Guy and how do we deal with him or her? Remember, you're tough. You sometimes must bite your tongue, let them do their thing, and then go in and make the deal happen the way it is supposed to happen. Remember, your job is not to be liked; your job is to make the company successful, which equals profitable! Mr. Nice Guy is for show, not at all in line with the Strategic Plan for company success. Ignore the inclination to complain about how Mr. Nice Guy treats others and focus, focus, focus on your role in the success of the Strategic Plan. As they say, keep your eye on the ball, and make Mr. Nice Guy look good. You can relish the knowledge that you have done your job and your best.

Remember—no more Mr. Nice Guy for you!

Business Fallacy #6: Outside Distractions— Good for Business?

All of us have what are considered outside distractions. Some of them are family issues, some are civic minded organizations, some are religious obligations, and some are business and professional organizations. Are these a benefit to business or a distraction?

That's entirely up to you. The business fallacy is that outside interests are good for business: socialize and get your name out there. For the boss, the "play golf" theory works up to a point.

What is that fine line between good for business and bad for business? It's the point when the distraction begins to overwhelm the boss's time or color their judgment about business issues such as utilizing employees to fulfill the needs of that outside distraction. That's BAD!!!

What do you do in this case? It's going to be very hard to tell the boss, your boss, that he needs to spend more time at the office OR he's making the wrong decisions based on his outside interests. At this point there is only one answer. Look for another job.

But, if you can deal with it, spend most of your efforts focused on the business, make the necessary decisions and show the results of your efforts. The more positive your results, the more decisions you will make and the more the boss will let go of the day-to-day operations. At that point you won't care how much time and energy he spends on outside interests. You will care how much this affects your paycheck because, at some point, you can showcase those positive results and make your pitch for a promotion and a raise.

Business Fallacy #7: Watch the Pennies and the Dollars

When I was a little girl, my daddy used to say, "Watch the pennies and the dollars will take care of themselves." I have lived my life with this philosophy, but is this the best theory for a successful business? I'm not sure. What I do know is, from observing those CEOs who blow up about every penny, they lose sight of the big picture and the dollars don't take care of themselves.

It's so easy to miss important pieces of the puzzle. Just because a small business owner requires that he see and sign every check or that he open the mail and prepared the bank deposit himself, doesn't mean he has control over the business practices of the company.

It's still possible to spend time on details and be considered an absentee owner. Absentee ownership can cause serious issues to arise and spin out of control. The agents of ownership will handle these issues, and decisions made by these agents could cause significant negative financial results. By the time owners gets their mind around what has happened, it's too little too late.

Major business decisions that impact profitability can also be made while ignoring the big picture. If all business factors not considered when making decisions, the decisions can be the beginning of significant failures. Part of the decision making process should include checking all references on consultants' previous successes and seeking input from management professionals within the organization. These are all necessary to make good business decisions.

Once again, it's your job to keep ownership involved and informed. You can't be Mr. Nice Guy and let the CEO or any other manager in the company make decisions that can hurt the company long-term. Your role is to guide the CEO to a set plan and implement the plan. Any deviation from that plan should be:

a. Documented
b. Discussed

c. Evaluated

d. Reviewed by ownership

e. Approved or disapproved in writing

f. Implemented or rejected

Only then can ownership maintain control of the dollars as well as the pennies.

Business Fallacy #8: Good Product Sells Itself

If this statement were true then how do you explain the success of the pet rock? It certainly wasn't a good product. You explain it with one word - marketing. Marketing is the key to the success of both a good product and a bad one. The bad ones will shake out and fade away in time like phases of the 70s, tie-dyes pants and the pet rock, but good products need good marketing in order to make them successful.

Innovation and good marketing are the ways to explain the success of Microsoft, Apple, Dell and IBM. Branding your good product can extend its life long enough for you to continue research and development to improve on what is working. That's the Intel solution. The first chips were fast, but compare that to the current generation—no comparison. You, the consumer, didn't even realize your computer was a work in progress, but

Intel did. The personal computer was a great innovation that utilized marketing talents to show consumers just how much they needed the product. Then, after you were hooked, those innovative companies just kept improving the work in progress, although your first computer worked just fine. Did it break before you bought your next computer? The answer is no. They just convinced you that you needed the computer to be faster, smarter and capable of more graphics than ever before. It's that talent for innovation and marketing that sells a good product. The most innovative computer system would go nowhere if no one ever knew about it.

The same thing is true for any company and its products, including your current employer. If the CEO of your company doesn't believe in new and innovative ways to market your product, you will eventually be outdone by your competition and your company will be out of business. Can you help? Yes. You don't need a marketing degree to use your awareness of business to guide the CEO to the right marketing ideas, talent, financial guidelines, and analysis of what works and what doesn't. Use your business sense to sell that good product rather than assume that A Good Product Sells Itself!

Appendix

Recommended Reading

I would not miss any of these authors' works. These are just a few that have played an important role in my progress toward success. I continue to learn each and every day, and search out teachers, mentors, and information that will help me grow in my life and my future. Take advantage of all that have come before you and learn from them.

***Good to Great* by Jim Collins, New York, New York: Harper Collins, 2001**—Jim Collins is an amazing author. Reading Good to Great is a good experience, but listening to Jim Collins tell you the story of Good to Great is a great experience. His powerful message is felt through his voice and passion for his material. Business management is not the most exciting subject but Mr. Collins combines business management with in-depth insight into the human spirit. This book inspires success.

Built To Last **by James C. Collins and Jerry I. Porras, New York, New York: Harper Collins, 1994**—Although this book was written prior to Good to Great is could qualify as a sequel. The knowledge you obtain from Good to Great is then expanded by your understanding of these lasting principles to apply to business and life issues.

The Success Principles **by Jack Canfield, New York, New York: Harper Collins, 2005**—Jack Canfield has captured story after story, and like Jim Collins, has a passion for the fundamental principles that permeate his message. Each principle, one by one, is accompanied by an inspirational story which makes the reader feel that they too can succeed if they apply the same principles in their life. I am a firm believer in listening to the message over and over again so purchase this book on CD. It's difficult to constantly remember why you should think positive and have hope for your future. Jack Canfield reminds you of that message each time you listen to a principle in this book.

The Five Temptations of A CEO: A Leadership Fable **by Patrick M. Lencioni, New York, New York, 1998**—The Leadership Fable series written by Patrick M. Lencioni are short stories with a message. If you are a CEO, or an aspiring leader, you should be reading all of the books in this series. The stories grab your interest and move quickly. When the story ends, the rest of the book helps you absorb the leadership message. From focus to teamwork to "Death by Meetings", we can all relate in some fashion. Don't miss any of this series.

The 21 Indispensable Qualities of A Leader **by John C. Maxwell, Nashville, Tennessee: Thomas Nelson, Inc., 1999**—John Maxwell has been teaching leadership skills for several years. He has refined the message down to 21 qualities of a leader that remind you that you have the ability to grow into a leader from wherever you stand in your life. Leadership is not a position, but a state of mind. The only way to know if you are a leader is to ask yourself these questions and give yourself honest answers.

Execution; The Discipline of Getting Things Done, by Larry Bossidy & Ram Charan, New York, New York, Crown Business, 2002— "Execution" is a blueprint for action. Theories are wonderful but at some point you must stop talking and actually do something. This book helps you to take action in your business environment. The ability to produce strategies that are successful comes from experience and research. This book is a must to assist you in taking your own experience and bringing research into action. When you understand these theories you can and will produce results.

WINNING **by Jack Welch with Suzy Welch, New York, New York: Harper Collins, 2005**—When you look to a winner for answers, you learn how to win. Jack Welch has experienced management at its finest and certainly gives you that understanding through this book. His plain spoken approach makes it simple to understand his message. If you listen to Mr. Welch as he presents his book on CD you can hear his quick wit and no excuses approach clearly in his voice. I always try to listen to those that have done it best, and this man has winning in his blood.

***The 8th HABIT; From Effectiveness to Greatness*, by Stephen R. Covey, New York, New York: Free Press, 2004—**I would call Stephen R. Covey the grandfather of all management material but I would be leaving out Dale Carnegie! Mr. Covey has provided material and programs from *The 7 Habits of Highly Effective People* to today's material in The 8th Habit for so many years. As a foundation for building your success habits a starting point would be the introspective view of yourself and your relationships that you receive when you really understand The 7 Habits. Once you have a true understanding of those habits you can move forward to The 8th Habit and apply yourself towards greatness. This can be a long and difficult journey and Mr. Covey is a great and patient guide.

ABOUT THE AUTHOR

As a young professional woman, Diane Dutton decided to think her way through the glass ceilings she discovered looming overhead. An MBA and CPA, she used her experiences, observations, and a plan to leave a trail of shattered glass behind her. In 26 years she has held the positions of Director of Finance and CFO, in public and private companies, and is currently CEO of CK Systemz, LLC, a start-up software development company she formed to help business professionals by providing break-thru patented interactive software solutions for Small Business.

Ms. Dutton credits Michael, her husband with nurturing her passion for success. She also credits her father, from whom she inherited her passion and her mother, from whom she inherited her guts. She has two great sons who have taught her the meaning of unconditional love. She puts all this together every day to achieve her goals.

A member of NAWBO, NAFE, and the AICPA, Ms. Dutton is the current Treasurer for the Nevada Society of CPAs, and Past President of the Las Vegas Chapter of the Nevada Society of CPAs. She is proud to be a CPA Ambassador 2006, representing the 360° of Financial Literacy program for the AICPA. She has also taught Accounting at UNLV, and seminars in Accounting and Tax for CPE Inc.

To Contact the Author:

Please visit www.writebookstoday.com to learn more about the Passion Statement and How to Break the Glass Ceiling in your life. If you have a desire to become an author, but never took the leap of faith, contact Diane directly to share your goals at:

ddutton@writebookstoday.com

LaVergne, TN USA
05 December 2009
166016LV00001B/37/A